The tu... yard ... of J. L. ... their foam ballast strip. *Brian Monaghan*

Overleaf: A front view of the goods shed at Dunnock Edge showing the surrounding buildings and outhouses etc. *Brian Monaghan*

£3.95

Model Railway

CONSTRUCTOR

Annual 1982

Edited by **S. W. Stevens-Stratten**

LONDON

IAN ALLAN LTD

First published 1981

ISBN 0 7110 1135 4

© Ian Allan Ltd 1981

Published by Ian Allan Ltd, Shepperton, Surrey;
and printed by Ian Allan Printing Ltd at their works
at Coombelands in Runnymede, England

Contents

Front cover: A scene on the 4mm scale Kingsbridge layout of the Wakefield Railway Modellers Society. *Brian Monaghan*

Back cover, top: A $\frac{3}{4}$ in scale model of the LNER Class A4 *Mallard* constructed in 1962 by H. Clarkson & Son of York.

Left: A view of Dunnock Edge station on the OO gauge layout of J. L. Flann. The goods shed is behind the platform. *Brian Monaghan*

M&GNR Loco No 9A

A 7mm fine scale model

DERYCK FEATHERSTONE

In the March '71 *MRC* the Editor published the second of three articles and drawings I had prepared of the smaller tank locos of the Midland and Great Northern Joint Railway. This article featured the Hudswell Clarke 4-4-0T locos as reboilered at Melton Constable.

Although I had one or two letters about the series of drawings, I have never heard that anyone was inspired to actually build one of the three types featured. The drawings were produced for my own modelling use in the first place, but for various reasons No 9A is the only one I have so far built and even then, it was not until 1975 that the almost complete model ran trials, in the all too familiar 'bare metal' state. Worse still, another four years elapsed before she finally emerged in the full glory of the intricately lined golden ochre livery and polished brass.

Below: Midland & Great Northern Railway loco No 9 in original livery. *Loco Publishing Co/Ian Allan Library*

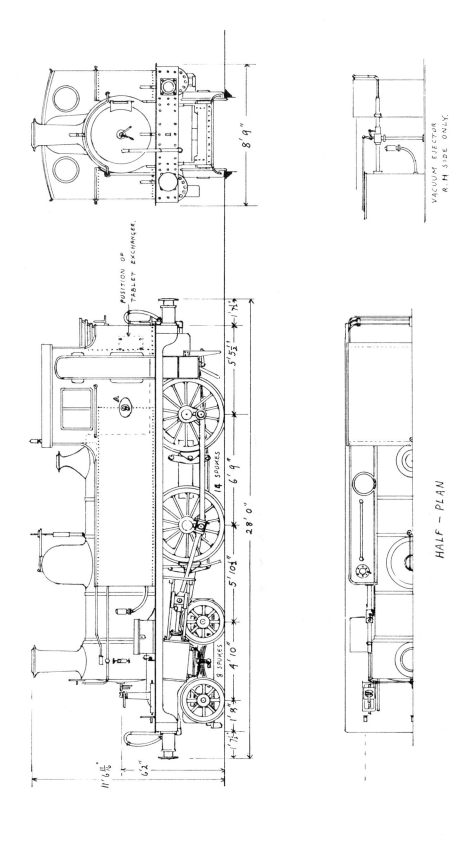

POSITION OF TABLET EXCHANGER.

14 SPOKES

8 SPOKES

VACUUM EJECTOR
R.H SIDE ONLY.

HALF – PLAN

8' 9"

11' 6¹¹⁄₁₆"

6' 2"

1' 7½"

1' 8"

4' 10"

5' 10¼"

6' 9"

5' 5½"

1' 7½"

28' 0"

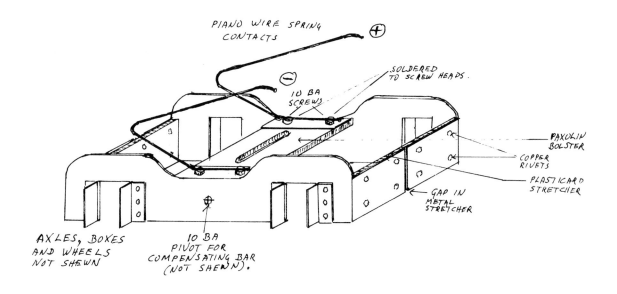

PIANO WIRE SPRING
CONTACTS

$\oplus$

$\ominus$

SOLDERED
TO SCREW HEADS.

10 BA
SCREWS

PAXOLIN
BOLSTER

COPPER
RIVETS

PLASTICARD
STRETCHER

GAP IN
METAL
STRETCHER

AXLES, BOXES
AND WHEELS
NOT SHEWN

10 BA
PIVOT FOR
COMPENSATING BAR
(NOT SHEWN).

INSULATED BOGIE FOR SPLIT AXLE PICK-UP.

(NOT TO SCALE)

I started the model in my usual way by turning the wheel castings. The eight-spoke, 2ft 9in dia bogie wheels were then obtainable in a long-discontinued range but I would not know where to look for such a product today.

At the time this engine was started our 'Wingham Branch' was still the stud-contact but, with an increasing circle of 2-rail friends, all new locos were being built convertible, with removable skates and change-over switches. Since then we too have gone 2-rail and the skates have been discarded.

Two of my pet theories for reliable running in 2-rail are to pick up current from as many wheels

as possible and to ensure firm rail contact by springing. This is more important in a small loco than a large one and No 9A uses all eight wheels for pick-up and is fully sprung.

The left-hand drivers are insulated by the well-known cut-and-Araldited spoke method and use a normal spring wire pick-up but the bogie is an experimental insulated axle job. These 'split axles' had been made to try a method described in an article published about that time — one of the great pleasures of the construction, (or 'scratch-building'), side of the hobby is this constant exchange of ideas. The bogie stretcher is $\frac{1}{18}$in Paxolin and the end plates are metal/Plastikard 'sandwiches', thus insulating the bogie down the centre. Springing, both downwards and sideways, is provided by two V-shaped spring steel wires, one on each side. These bear on deeply slotted brass contacts on the Paxolin mainframe stretcher. The right hand one is earthed to the frames and the left to the insulated pick-up block. Excess sideplay of the bogie is controlled by a normal centre pin and slot in the bolster.

Opposite and below: The author's completed gauge O fine scale model of M&GNR 4-4-0T No 9A.

The bogie is of the 'Adams' type with springs and equalising bars outside the frames and on the model the springs are dummy, one side being fixed while the other has about 1mm up and down movement, pivoting on the equalising bar. This is an effective way of providing 3-point suspension which I have used on several other bogie engines.

The mainframes of the loco are 30thou nickel-silver and the stretchers are Paxolin blocks machined true in the lathe, (you've got to be really good with a file to do this by hand!). The horn blocks are soldered and riveted. Following the advice of Geoff Pember, I never trust solder alone for a job like this. The rivets are pieces of copper wire hammered into holes drilled after

soldering and slightly countersunk on each side. Excess copper is filed off afterwards. Care is needed not to overdo the hammering, riveting is a very satisfying kind of job and it is easy to get 'carried away' and distort the frames.

Axleboxes are made of $\frac{3}{8}$in square brass bar centred, drilled and parted off on a home made collet in the lathe, an excellent idea for which I am indebted to Mr E. J. Cooke via an article in the *Gauge O Guild Gazette*.

The motor is a Romford Bulldog, using a 40:1 gear. Actually, with this motor I should have used a 50:1 as a 7mm scale 4ft $7\frac{1}{2}$in driving wheel is quite large for a small OO motor. Today there is a wider choice of motor than when I started this

Above: The completed model with M&GNR 6-wheel brake van — the latter made by Peter Featherstone.

Opposite: The completed model on the Hillmorton Branch line in gauge O belonging to Peter Featherstone.

model and I could probably get something a bit bigger in. Even so, No 9A easily handles four 6-wheel carriages and she is not over-fast.

As the driving wheels are sprung the motor is mounted on a brass sub-frame or gearbox enclosing the driving axle, in technical circles I think this is called 'nose hung'.

The body is chiefly nickel-silver, with turned brass fittings. Special care had to be taken with the dome and safety-valve cover as they are left bright and in the prototype they had a mirror finish. Buffer heads and cylinder end covers are mild steel and also highly polished.

My indispensable Bedford rivet tool produced the mass of rivet heads round the tank sides and

tops. I may be accused of rivet-counting, (not for the first time), but it really is important to get these about the right size and spacing in any scale of model, otherwise it is far better to leave them off altogether.

For a small loco there were quite a few tricky jobs, for example, not only are the tank and bunker tops and corresponding edges of the cab finished with half-round beading but the spectacle plates are recessed about 2in from the edges of the cab sides. Soldering these called for the careful use of card packing pieces and quite a bit of luck. The beading was soldered on before assembling the cab-tank-bunker unit with these pieces pinned to a board and the corners formed round nails or dowel pegs of suitable sizes.

The two lifting jacks carried by this class and the Beyer-Peacock 4-4-0 tender engines of the M&GNR were fabricated from brass strip and I2BA screws, with turned columns. During construction they would actually work but I strongly resisted the play value of such a gimmick and they are now immovably fixed to the running plate. If one is to encourage, or even allow, young

9

people, (in my case, grandsons), to run the railway responsibly I think it is essential to avoid fitting working brakes, opening toolboxes and manually operated jacks, cranes, watertanks etc. These are a natural and irresistible temptation to little fingers. It is unfair and discouraging to young enthusiasts to have to keep saying 'Don't'. (End of sermon, back to the model).

A full set of cab and backhead fittings was installed including the unusual vertical handbrake wheel, resembling a small ship's wheel. The cab roof was left a tight push fit to enable these fittings to be looked at occasionally, (OK, I know about 'little fingers'). It is very difficult to see anything through the cab openings as they are a bare $\frac{1}{8}$in (8.25mm) wide. This might present a problem to some ASLEF members today, but photographs confirm that obesity was not a condition that many pre-grouping loco men suffered from, (or could afford to enjoy?).

Some photographs show that the locomotive was fitted with Whittaker's tablet apparatus on both sides, for forward or reverse running, for part of its career. This is obviously a modified version for tank locos but I have no drawing and could not produce one from the photos. If reliable information comes to hand it should be possible to add these fittings later.

After a long running-in period in bare metal I managed to spray paint a reasonable representation of the elusive golden ochre colour. By trial and error I mixed my own paint as the trade version seemed too yellow, more like the famous Stroudley 'Improved Engine Green'. I used a drop or two of scarlet and sienna in yellow ochre until it looked right, at least to my eyes and those of a friend who knew M&GNR locos well. It is that bit of red that gives it that lovely glowing tint.

When it came to lining and lettering my nerve failed me and 9A was put aside for another long period. Eventually with the help of my good friend Barrie Walls, of 'Wallsea' layout fame, it went to Alan Brackenborough to be finished professionally. Never was money better spent, Alan's artistry has captured the charm of the prototype to perfection.

Looking at the model, one marvels at an age that could create such elegance in metal and such beauty of finish basically to perform the humdrum functions of branch line service on a struggling minor railway. It is small wonder that

Above: An M&GNR ballast train at Bramley Junction on the Wingham Branch layout. The brake van and the ex-NER wagons were built by Jim Featherstone.

Opposite: A view of a sister loco — No 10 with Pullman type clerestory coach.
Loco Publishing Co/Ian Allan Library

the perceptive eye of the Grand Old Man, Mr William Marriot, engineer, locomotive superintendent and, later, general manager of the M&GNR should single out this little beauty as his favourite locomotive. She was usually chosen not only for official trips in the special inspection saloon but also for family outings to the seaside, (in that same saloon), on the great man's birthday. After all, today's top brass run about in the company's chauffer driven car or the executive jet. Given the choice, I would have preferred little 9A and a six-wheel saloon, wouldn't you?

Now, where's that drawing of the M&GN inspection saloon?

Bridges – 1

A Photo-feature from the camera of BRIAN MONAGHAN

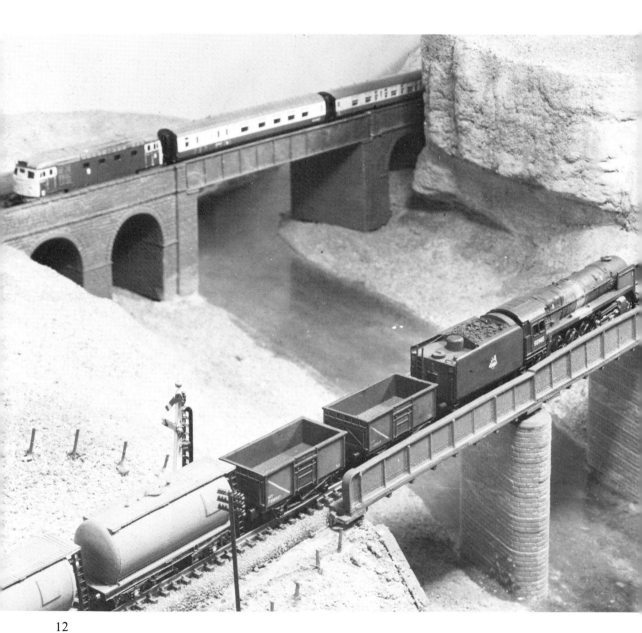

Opposite: A model of a plate-girder bridge on stone piers which crosses a river on the N gauge layout of the Sutton Coldfield MRC.

Above: The 4mm scale layout of Ken Northwood features this large viaduct crossing the Torrey Valley. It is constructed in deal and balsa wood with Faller embossed stone paper facing. The loco is a K's kit with Pittman motor in the tender with flexible drive to the coupled wheels. The firebox is filled with lead to keep centre of gravity further to the rear.

13

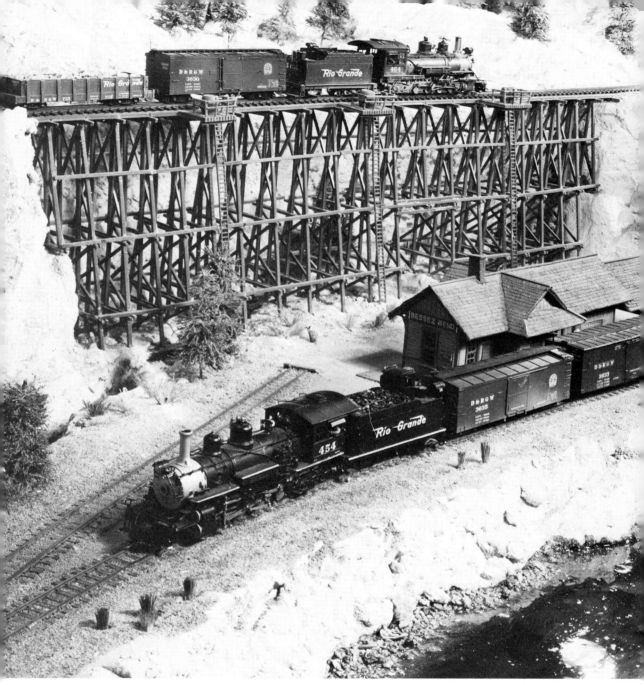

Above: A trestle bridge which is mainly built from a Heljan plastic kit on the HOn3 American layout of John Porter. The loco in the foreground is a PFM model, while the one on the bridge is a Westside model.

Opposite upper: A wooden trestle bridge on the O gauge layout of the West Lancashire O Gauge Group. An aerial ropeway is in the top background.

Opposite lower: An LMSR streamlined Pacific in 4mm scale crosses a viaduct on a section of R. F. Taylor's layout which depicts the scenery of the Settle-Carlisle line.

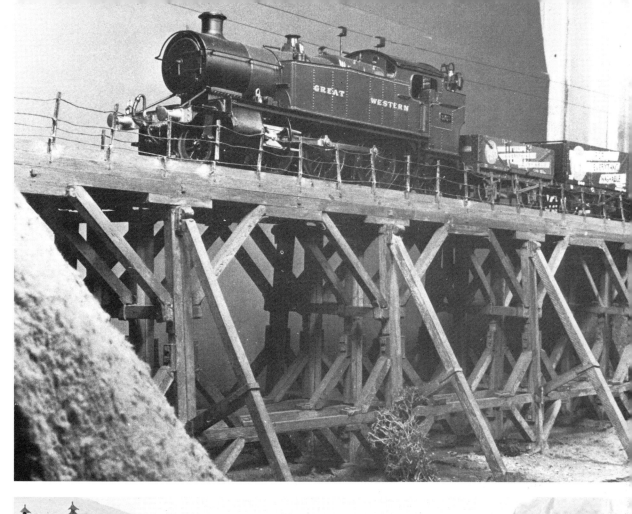

Opposite upper: A lattice girder bridge on the 4mm scale layout of R. F. Taylor.

Opposite lower: A river bridge on the 4mm scale Highfield-on-Sea and Pen-y-Ffordd layout of the Whitchurch (Cardiff) and District Model Engineering Society.

Above: A 3.5mm scale model of Widnes Viaduct and part of West Bank Docks as a diorama created by the late Jack Nelson.

Left: An ex-Hornby tinplate O gauge model of LNER D49 class No 201 *Bramham Moor* crosses a 6ft long bridge, actually made of wood, on the 'Craven and Ravenstone' garden layout of W. K. B. Clarke.

Below: A delightful overbridge on an interesting Narrow Gauge layout.

Opposite upper: A Dean Goods crosses a plate girder bridge as it comes off the branch line on the 4mm scale Blackhill Line of Howard Lobb. *R. Gordon Taylor*

Opposite lower: A simple trestle bridge on a Narrow Gauge layout. *Ron Prattley*

Scenic Development of a Simple O Gauge Layout

An English style layout in the USA

VAUGHAN SPARHAM

Vaughan Sparham, (A member of the Gauge O Guild) resident in the USA since 1972, describes his planning and development of an indoor O gauge scenic Midland Railway period layout with some local (US) materials and accessories.

Obviously, an illusion of space is less difficult to achieve in N gauge or OO gauge but, by virtue of scale, the creation of spatial illusions in O gauge must be differently approached. On a raised O gauge layout, eye level is about at tree-top height with consequent effects on the importance of detailed ground feature modelling. Trains in O gauge will also be viewed passing through surrounding trees and scenery while they would be seen passing under the trees and over the scene in N scale.

Scale Relationships

Indoor O scale scenics in the USA enjoy the more generous dimensions of so much of American domestic accommodation. Almost all suburban houses have basements which often provide a nearly unbroken area 30ft long and up to 30ft in width. At about $18\frac{1}{2}$sq ft/O scale acre, this represents a total area of up to 48 scale acres.

The baseboard area of a typical American basement layout can provide about $\frac{3}{4}$/scale route mile of oval single-line track. Observation and operating wells (with optional access through hinged or lifting sections) often have an equivalent area of about five scale acres each. The limitations of available scale vertical height should also be taken into account at the planning stage. The normal floor to ceiling height in an American basement is 8ft. With a baseboard raised to about 3ft 3in, in practice only about three usable feet are available for above-track landscape features; this translates into about 150 scale feet of elevation.

Landscape Design

Working within these constraints, careful landscape design is important especially with spring-driven or live-steam locomotives which really require a dead-level path if they are to operate satisfactorily. it is, thus, necessary to confine all variations in level strictly to the topography which surrounds the track.

Be it a typical natural history museum diorama or the Derby Museum O scale MR exhibition layout, indoor representations of three dimensional scenery must achieve a convincing 'jump' from the foreground to the background. Even with excellent art work, this can be difficult to manage without convenient hedgerows, rows of skyline trees or skyline boundary walls or fences to justify those sharp breaks in the perspective which help to create the essential illusion of scenic depth. It is better if the foreground does not appear just as a scenic corridor or culvert through which model trains pass back and forth. A background is far more convincing when some features other than plain sky are depicted. To develop a convincing topography it is effective to suggest that the ground drops away not far from the other side of the tracks from most viewpoints. The well-known W. S. Norris layout and the more recent Bromford and High Peak, also in O gauge, exploited this technique. The Derby

Opposite upper: General view of the Southern half of the layout and overlooking 480ft platform (actually 10ft) of the branch line terminus.

Opposite lower: A rebuilt Hornby Compound in a wooded section of the layout.

Museum layout does not show this so well and, in my opinion, its scenery is rather the less convincing as a consequence.

Value of Curvature

Whether landscape gardening or creating a diorama (and the late Jack Nelson was just as significant an artist in dioramic perspective as ever was John Ahern with his undistorted and now preserved Madder Valley Line (in the equally wellknown Pendon Railway Museum at Long Wittenham), curvature is an essential ingredient for natural or contrived landscaping. It creates the illusion of enlarging any given space. O gauge scenic design has to be particularly resourceful because of the scale's greed for space indoors.

Buildings

Under the Lionel mark in the USA, much of the locomotive and rolling stock in O gauge strongly resembles a good (and, sometimes, not so good) tinplate model of the 1930s. By contrast, a somewhat transient range of far more beautifully

Above: The provender mill with live steam 4-4-2 doing some shunting.

Opposite upper: Close-up of the overbridge leading from station yard to village (not yet modelled) with feed mill and siding.

Opposite lower: The road to the station.

detailed Lionel O gauge plastic kits of buildings and structures continues to be available. With a little careful trimming or painting (and some rearrangement) these can be convincingly Anglicised for use on period layouts. All the buildings illustrated are from this Lionel range and all represent brick or clapboard construction.

One of the few practical disadvantages in American O scale modelling is the inconsistent

22

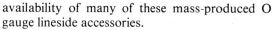

availability of many of these mass-produced O gauge lineside accessories.

Manufacturers' patterns of production must necessarily be dictated by management accountants. Were this not so, both the quality and variety of products here in the US would probably suffer.

Both the British and American toy markets have basic demands for items like track and beginners' train sets. However, amongst life-time modellers there are other distinct markets for any new item introduced. It can be bought to improve established layouts, of as a component for a first (or new) project. And while life-time modellers have their needs, youthful train set users (with less exacting tastes) also need to be attracted and satisfied at very different levels and prices.

There are also the speculative collectors. The Lionel range offers annually a special limited edition, gift-boxed O gauge train. Many are bought by collectors never to be used but only stored in mint condition for their investment potential. By British standards of fine scale modelling in O gauge, these are very coarse models reminiscent of Hornby and Basset-Lowke merchandise of the early 1930s.

Above left: Modified lineside hut from a plastic kit.

Above: End view of modifed Lionel engine-shed kit.

So obviously, before launching any new product the manufacturer must consider the broadest possible appeal and the most rapid return on investment. Hence marketing seems to lean toward the limited edition philosophy.

Appreciating these distinctions can help the dedicated O scale modeller to understand why so many items from the American market illustrated in the accompanying photographs were short-lived and hence purchased on sight, but others will surely take their place. Even recent catalogues can become obsolete within 6 months of the publication date and perhaps this is why the well-known firm of Walthers in Milwaukee does not appear to carry the Lionel range at all in their $\frac{1}{2}$in thick O gauge catalogue published from time to time.

Apart from this, there are several manufacturers other than Lionel which currently

24

offer O scale buildings, but all seem far beyond adaptation to the British railway architectual conventions of the days of steam and were therefore not considered.

However, by special arrangement (and with the usual disclaimers) Nworb's Hobby House of Columbus, Ohio has consented to accept British enquiries for a Lionel accessory list if accompanied by a ready-addressed envelope and a cheque for $1 sent c/o 5832 Place de la Concorde West, Columbus, Ohio 43229, USA (which enables British cheques to be taken). Orders could only be accepted subsequently on the clear understanding that if the merchandise is out of stock, money would have to be refunded, by return.

Below: The Lionel engine-shed slightly modified and hand painted.

Forestation and Tree Construction

Forestation is an important feature in almost any landscape. In O scale, the foreground is seen in greater detail than in smaller scales and thus its being well modelled is that much the more significant. Due to the lower effective viewing angle in O scale, trees can be very important in suggesting the illusion of depth in the scene. Trains passing through wooded area can be temporarily obscured and revealed as they move through their natural surroundings.

It is the intimate contrast between the natural and the mechanical which is such an important ingredient of the railway image which fascinates many enthusiasts. This does well to be emphasised.

Options for using commercially available trees were carefully reviewed. A few existing commercial products were/are suitable but are not really varied or large enough for O gauge. The great need is for tree construction to be rapid and

Above: The new station which has been created from three Lionel freight station kits.

inexpensive — something between 12 and 18 trees per hour if the task is not to become too boring, expensive or demanding of limited modelling time.

After some realistic consideration, it was decided that for the projected layout, even only the smaller half as illustrated, before a removal demanded dismantling, would require about 200 trees. I think a fair US/UK camparison would be for the average cost of materials to approximate 10p per tree. 12in and 6in polyethylene plastic foliage had certain useful properties — gentle wilting by warming produced a variety of realistic shapes. Most seemed to resemble elms and/or

26

After a few seconds of agitation, the polyethylene tree is removed from the bag with the foliage firmly adhering to the basic structure shape. After about 15 minutes, batches of trees are sprayed with Colonial Green aerosol paint and then lightly dusted with a strong yellow spray paint. The trunk section is sprayed with a puff of dark, flat brown paint. All can then be left to dry for a few minutes.

The tree trunk is completed with a cut length of hollow (tubular) braided or woven brown shoe lace and the tree is complete.

Obviously, colours can be spray-blended to the very yellow-green of the early spring — the darker, mature green of summer, or the brilliance of a deciduous autumn foliage, if such is preferred.

General Upbuild of the Scene

Trees in profusion are obviously a convincing cloak to mantle the otherwise rather stark groundscape which itself was worked up from very cheap felt carpeting — some even second-hand.

Spraying with adhesive, sprinkled with dry-as-dust soil, sands, grit and even small stones simulates the sparse grazing of the marginal farm in hill country.

Hedges where needed, were worked up from aquarium filter floss, spray-glued and scattered with sawdust before spray colouring.

My conclusion was that even an O gauge layout (fitted into a 27ft by 15ft portion of the basement of an American ranch-style house) could be fully cloaked in a lush rural and British setting at a total cost comparable to that of the O gauge 4-4-2 live-steam Tilbury Tank which now could prettily pick its path from station to station between limestone walls and cliffs, grazing land and those quiet untrodden copses which typified the more remote areas where Midland metals once ran through their Derbyshire dales: and all the scenic raw materials were obtained from the local Woolworths!

sycamores in the 12in size, and a thorn or apple type of tree in the 6in versions. These, of course, represent about 45ft in height and 24ft in height, respectively. A little later, an appropriate polyethylene frond was discovered, which, when warmed and drooped while hold trunk-uppermost over a gas or electric ring, added a very credible poplar tree to the range. Using somewhat similar techniques, some while later, an ideal conifer was developed by similarly manipulating the branch tips of man-sized plastic Christmas trees or medium sized bottle brushes, both with wire stems. Regardless of the origins of the four different varieties, (tall deciduous, fruit or thorn trees, poplars and conifers), all can subsequently be drenched in photographer's-mount spray-adhesive. The actual foliage is mouse or hamster litter or alteratively, fine sawdust for the conifers. It has applied to the adhesive-sodden polyethylene tree by shaking the tree in a brown paper bag $\frac{1}{4}$ full of the litter.

27

The Pattishall Quarry Railway

A freelance Narrow Gauge System

J. NEIL HELSBY

The Pattishall Quarry started life along with many other Northamptonshire ironstone quarries in the nineteenth century. The first ironstone was quarried from fields known locally as Foster's Booth to the west of Pattishall. The ore was originally transhipped the two miles to the London-Birmingham railway by horse and cart. The Pattishall Quarry was a relatively small affair and its days seemed numbered once railway lines began to appear within quarry boundaries.

The directors of the Pattishall Quarry recognised that neither the ironstone field nor the Company was large enough to support a normal railway. The successful laying of a 2ft 6in gauge line at the nearby Storefield Ironstone

Quarries spurred the Pattishall Quarry to follow suit. Fortunately, the main line was only two miles away making a link to it near Bugbrooke feasible. So it was that the Pattishall Quarry Railway came into existence. The line from Foster's Booth to the exchange sidings following the river along most of its route. The only major

Below: Ryde pilots *Blue Peter* on an enthusiasts day special.

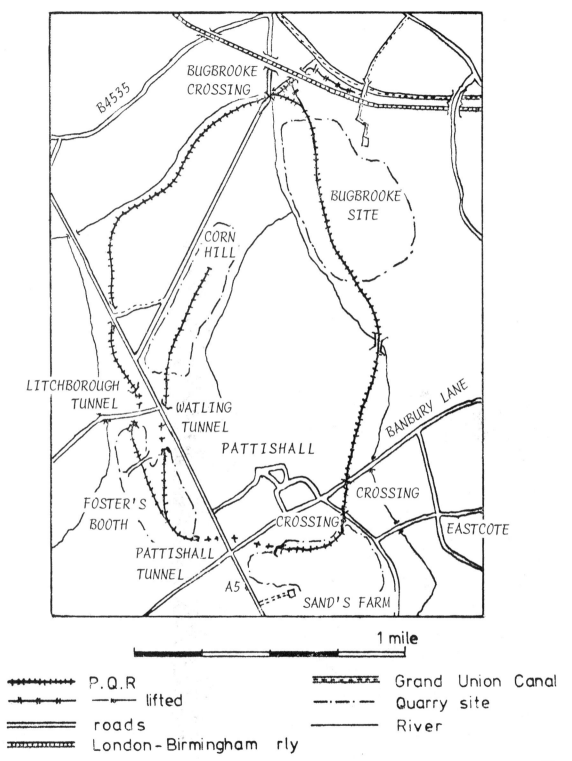

1 mile

	P.Q.R		Grand Union Canal
	lifted		Quarry site
	roads		River
	London-Birmingham rly		

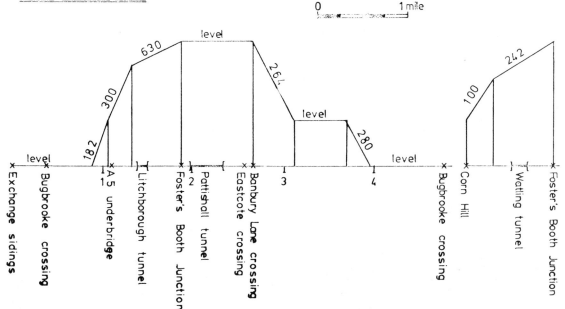

P.Q.R gradient profile

0 ⊢━━━━━━━┤ 1 mile

630 · 300 · 182 · level · level · Exchange sidings · Bugbrooke crossing · A 5 underbridge · 1 · Litchborough tunnel · Foster's Booth Junction · 2 · Pattishall tunnel · Banbury Lane crossing · Eastcote crossing · 264 · 3 · level · 280 · 4 · level · Bugbrooke crossing · 100 · Corn Hill · 242 · Watling tunnel · Foster's Booth Junction

engineering works were the 200 yard Litchborough tunnel and the bridge taking the line under the A5. The Grand Union Canal conveniently runs alongside the exchange sidings, giving the Company the option of barge or railway to carry the ore further afield. The railway line was opened in due course with a gathering of noblemen and gentry. The first official train, leaving to a fanfare of trumpets, consisted of four side tip wagons pulled by the 0-4-0 steam loco *Ryde* (named after the chairman of the board).

Thereafter, the quarry and railway settled down to a number of years of prosperity. As the ore in Foster's Booth was giving out, the Bugbrooke and Sand's Farm sites were opened. Inability to buy the land giving direct rail access from the new sites, forced the Company to build the Pattishall tunnel under the A5 to join up at Foster's Booth. Finally the Corn Hill fields were

Opposite: Ryde leaves Litchborough tunnel and emerges into the sunlight.

Top: Another view of Ryde leaving the tunnel with the Directors saloon.

Above: Blue Peter with the first train of the day passes under Foster's footbridge.

purchased and once more building the railway became a problem. Eventually the Watling Tunnel was constructed to bring the line back to Foster's Booth. This route into Foster's Booth would have required a run round loop to be constructed. Since the short comings of only one locomotive had been apparent for some time, it was decided to purchase a second one. This would also dispense with a difficult track layout at Foster's Booth. The availability of a second-hand loco encouraged this approach. This loco was an earlier version of Ryde virtually identical except in having no driver's cab. The directors having long since tired of the railway novelty, the new engine received neither name nor number. A few years later, when internal combustion become the vogue, two diesel 0-4-0 machines were obtained.

As the Bugbrooke site was enlarged, the railway moved onwards until it eventually became possible to make a connection at Bugbrooke crossing. This gave trains an easier route to the main line and consequently the section from Foster's Booth through Litchborough Tunnel was used infrequently. Internal combustion again played a part when the econ-omics of lorries made main line rail transport redundent. A new yard with a tipping dock was built at Bugbrooke crossing and the rail head exchange sidings were duly lifted.

Several unspectacular years followed until the general decline in the ironstone industry in the 1920s. Scraping through this period, the quarry plodded on until finally it was bought up by the

Opposite upper: Blue Peter on mixed traffic duties.

Opposite lower: The same loco on passenger train passes Foster's Booth.

Above: Ryde on an unusual duty — pulling empty side tip wagons.

George Ernest Organisation (GEO). Modern diesel trucks being capable of driving readily to the quarry face, the railway was ripe for abandonment. Fortunately, one of the new GEO directors was a railway enthusiast and he persuaded the board not to scrap the rail facilities. Little happened to the railway however for a couple of years except, that is, for the slow decay caused to wagons and rail exposed to the elements and the damage to the locomotives when the engine shed collapsed one windy night.

A number of local railway enthusiasts eventually got together with the GEO director and formed a preservation society. Work commenced on restoring the track and motive power. Foster's Booth being of no interest to the new quarry owners, initial effort was concentrated here. The GEO had *Ryde* put into working order

and she was returned to the line resplendent in her original PQR green livery and brass nameplate. Meanwhile, one of the diesels was rebuilt by the enthusiasts. The original bodywork was severely damaged and had to be scrapped but fortunately the chassis was in good condition. The new body shell was designed for the loco and allows three people to travel in the cab. An open platform enabled sleepers, ballast, etc, to be carried. This arrangement saved a lot of effort in wagon shunting. During the course of reconstruction, the loco became nicknamed *Batchelors Button*, the name it eventually carried when turned out in its new orange and yellow livery. The quarry had never carried passengers (officially) and so the new society had to set about rebuilding wagons and vans to enable fee paying day members to be carried safely. Consequently two bogie coaches were built. These coaches utilised the chassis from old ore wagons as the basis of the bogies. A steel girder underframe with wooden planking formed the coach floor. Seats were bolted to this to provide a fifteen seat coach. The first trip behind *Ryde* through Pattishall Tunnel showed up the flaws in the system; a roof and end screen were added immediately. In contrast to the GEOs green livery, the society's stock was painted blue and white. Meanwhile, the GEO had purchased two bogie coaches from a famous continental railway and had them completely refurbished. They presently appeared on the line and quickly

Above: Sun Chariot on quarry business pulling the explosives van.

Left: Batchelors Button leaves Watling tunnel on permanent way business.

became known as the director's saloons, additional 1st class fares being levied on those sampling the plush interiors.

As the line prospered, so the track mileage was reclaimed and stock overhauled. The second diesel was rebuilt on the same lines as Batchelors Button so Sun Chariot differed only in that the platform was built with sides and a bench seat. The additional safety that this afforded the per-manent way gang was obvious and Batchelors Button was modified accordingly. The second steam loco was eventually repaired by the efforts of Society members. Appropriately named after the GEO director who saved the railway, Blue Peter appears in blue lined white. Over the years, the line has imported additional four wheel passenger stock and rebuilt many of the original wagons and vans. The old junction at Bugbrooke crossing has been rebuilt to turn the line into a $4\frac{1}{4}$ mile circuit. With the recent completion of this work, effort is now directed on the Corn Hill branch. Corn Hill will be the eventual site of the storage sheds and repair shop. The diesel tanks, currently on the site of the original engine shed at Foster's Booth, will also be moved to Corn Hill.

Regular week-end steam services now take place providing an interesting afternoon for visitors. The only official duties now performed by the railway for the quarry is in shifting explosives in the special gun powder van between sites.

The photographs of the Pattishall Quarry Railway around Foster's Booth show the state of the model to date. Finally, I would like to apologise to the worthy people of Pattishall and district who have hitherto been unaware of the quarries and railway around them.

Railway Construction Requirements

Full size dimensions reduced for the Modeller

J. G. GLOVER

Government regulation of the construction and operation of the railways is almost as old as the railways themselves. Formerly the province of the Board of Trade, the department of Transport is now responsible. The last issue of the *Railway Construction and Operation Requirements for Passenger Lines and Recommendations for Goods Lines of the Minister of Transport* was published in 1950 and is now in the process of being updated. However, certain of the Requirements relating to structural and electrical clearances have already been revised, and the following is a summary of them as far as they affect modellers. Correctness in these matters, as others, is bound to contribute to the overall effect of the model railway.

The new structural clearances are to be provided on new lines and on existing railways whenever reconstruction takes place. They have been specifically designed to cater for 200kmph (125mph) running, and are entirely metricated. The clearances shown in the Diagram are for straight and level track, and will require widening on curves, depending on their radius. It should perhaps be pointed out that many dimensions are advisory rather than obligatory, and may be reduced with the consent of the Railway Inspectorate. Where clearances are reduced, special warning signs to staff will often be required.

Permitted infringements of the structure gauge below platform level include ground signals, bridge girders, etc. Above the tracks, all wires and cables (telephone, electricity, etc) must be at least 6000mm above rail level.

Where there are more than two running lines, an extra 1200mm must be allowed between each pair of running lines; a siding adjacent to a running line should have not less than 4300mm between their respective centre lines.

Clearances for overhead line equipment have also been revised. In the case of 25kv AC systems (the British standard), the contact wire should normally be 4315mm above rail level, the absolute minimum clearance being 4165mm. At public level crossings the height is raised to 5600mm. All these clearances must be observed under the worst conditions of temperature and loading. Supports for overhead equipment may infringe the structure gauge but must not be less than 2185mm from the centre line of the nearest track.

An increased height to the structure gauge is also required with a standard clearance of 4780mm above rail level. The minimum clearance is 4350mm.

Right: This view of a Southern Region 4VEP unit (Class 423) at Clapham Junction shows well why clearances have to be increased on curves. The train is travelling at about 15mph. *J. G. Glover*

It is important to ensure the safety of men working on the track by providing them with means to stand clear of passing trains. Higher speeds have added to these difficulties, and the Requirements relating to Refuges have also been revised. The clearance required between the centre line of the nearest running line and any fixed obstruction of a continuous length of 40 metres or more is 2340mm, rising to 3210mm where speeds of 161-200km/h (101-125mph) are envisaged. Fixed obstructions include bridge sides, retaining walls and cuttings, and buildings.

If the required clearances are not available on either side of the line, Refuges have to be provided.

A Refuge must be not less than 2000mm high, 1400mm wide, and 700mm deep. Where there are two or more running lines, Refuges are located at not less than 40 metre intervals on both sides of the tracks and staggered to give an effective spacing of 20 metres. On single lines, all the Refuges may be on the same side of the line, again to give a 20 metre spacing.

It should be noted that while the new require-

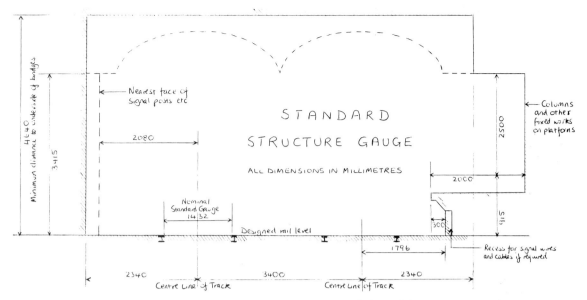

STANDARD

STRUCTURE GAUGE

ALL DIMENSIONS IN MILLIMETRES

Opposite: Many Southern Region lines had limited clearance and the ex-SECR lines are some of the worst. On the Hastings route, special narrow stock is provided; this view of an up Hastings train (Class 202 diesel-electric multiple unit) entering Tonbridge shows why. *J. G. Glover*

ments for Refuges are generally only mandatory in respect of new lines or reconstruction, they are also obligatory when the line speed is increased above 160km/h. Refuge provision is thus one of the many tasks which have to be undertaken before HST operation is introduced.

It might be thought that these clearances have application only to the ultra-modern image layout. However, bridge and other reconstruction has for many years taken into account the need for increased electrical clearances in particular, even if there was no immediate prospect of the line being electrified. To a large extent therefore, the Requirements merely confirm the Department's approval for the existing situation. These clearances therefore might be incorporated for 'new' structures in any models set in the period of the last 20 years.

Readers wanting further information are advised to consult the *Railway Construction and Operation Requirements — Structural and Electrical Clearances* published for the Department of Transport by HMSO, and on which this article is based.

All dimensions in the text and in the diagram are quoted in millimetres, actual size. A conversion table for 7mm, 4mm and 2mm scales is given below.

Actual size mm	Equivalent size in millimetres: 7mm scale	4mm scale	2mm scale
300	7	4	2
700	16	9	5
915	21	12	6
1200	28	16	8
1400	32	18	9
1432	33	19	9
1796	41	24	12
2000	46	26	13
2080	48	27	14
2185	50	29	14
2340	54	31	15
2500	57	33	16
3210	74	42	21
3400	78	45	22
3415	78	45	22
4165	96	55	27
4300	99	56	28
4315	99	57	28
4350	100	57	29
4640	107	61	30
4780	110	63	31
5600	129	73	37
6000	138	79	39
20m	459	262	131
40m	919	525	262

BR Standard Steam Locomotives

A brief survey for the Modeller

PETER KAZMIERCZAK

With the interest currently being shown in BR diesel and electric power, let us not forget that since Nationalisation a large number of steam locomotives have also been built. Many were to pre-1948 designs, being a continuation of the construction of LMSR, SR and GWR types, but a series of twelve Standard classes were also built. It is these Standard locomotives, of which 999 were built between 1951-60, that I want to look at from a modeller's viewpoint. For those who want further details I have listed some of the more useful books and magazines in the bibliography.

Many of these types lasted right up to the end of steam in August 1968 and I have drawn a diagram which illustrates the life span of the BR Standard classes. Looking at this diagram it will be seen that the class 7, 4-6-2s, for example, were built between 1951 and 1954 and withdrawn during the period from 1965-68. On the other hand the Class 3, 2-6-0s did not appear until 1954 and were withdrawn between 1965-67. Thus supposing your layout was set in 1953, then you could run 'Britannias' and 'Clans' but not the 9Fs. Alternatively, if you modelled the 1967

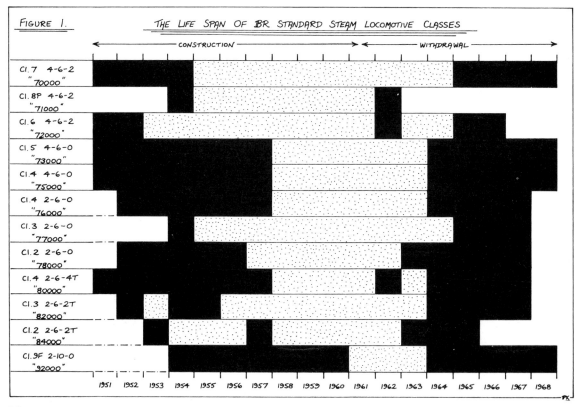

FIGURE I. THE LIFE SPAN OF BR STANDARD STEAM LOCOMOTIVE CLASSES

Above: BR Standard Class 7 No 70000 in black livery straight from the works before going on trials and before the nameplate 'Britannia' was added. *BR*

Below: Class 7 No 70018 *Flying Dutchman* in BR livery. This loco spent much of its days on the Western Region. Note footholds in smoke-deflectors. *F. W. Day*

about things like that. If one wants to run certain types of motive power together why not. To be honest, on my own layout, I sometimes run a Canadian Pacific Bo-Bo diesel in place of one of my Class 20s when the fancy takes me. Before I digress too much, let us consider each of BRs 12 standard classes.

Class 7 4-6-2 70000

Better known as the 'Britannias' these have always been a popular class with modellers. Currently available from the trade in 4mm scale is the Hornby model (now updated), while Minitrix manufacture one for N gauge. Both these models would form the basis of a really super-detailed representation of the class. Many

period you could operate Class 5 and Class 4 4-6-0s but not 'Clans' and Class 2, 2-6-2Ts. However, there is little point in being dogmatic about which locos could or could not run a layout at a particular time; life is too short to worry

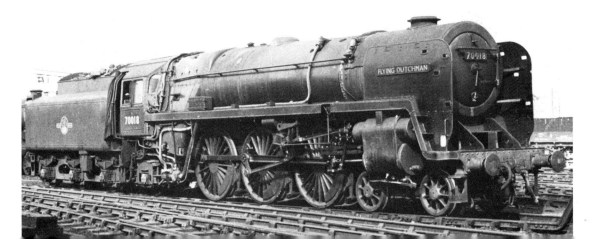

Above: Class 5 4-6-0 — a popular class on BR. *BR*

Opposite upper: The only loco built in Class 8P, the *Duke of Gloucester* photographed as it emerged from the Works. *BR*

Opposite centre: Only ten of Class 6 were built and all worked in the North of England and Scotland. *BR*

Opposite lower: Another view of a Class 6 — No 72009 *Clan Stewart. Loco Publishing Co*

years ago Tri-ang made a TT gauge version, while Trix made a model to 3.8mm scale — both these items occasionally appear on the secondhand market.

As regards the prototype, 55 were constructed with the Nos 70000 — 70054. The last ten were built with the larger BRID type tender which, appearance wise is the most significant variation within the class. In the 1950s these locos worked on many routes hauling such crack expresses as the 'Golden Arrow' out of Victoria and many of the Paddington-South Wales workings. Their particular niche and one route which they will always be associated was the London Liverpool Street-Norwich. In the 1960s the increased dieselisation, the 'Britannias' appeared on more freight workings and eventually all were con-

centrated on the West Coast Main Line working north of Crewe on all manner of duties.

For those modelling the transition period from steam to diesel in the North of England this loco class is a 'must'.

Class 8P 4-6-2 71000

The solitary *Duke of Gloucester* No 71000 was the last express passenger loco to be built in Britain. It spent virtually its entire life on the West Coast route working out of Crewe North Shed.

As there was only one member in the class it is not suprising that no models are available from the trade. It may be possible to modify one of the proprietary versions of the 'Britannia' class by extending the firebox by a scale foot, modifying the valve gear and fitting a double chimney.

Class 6 4-6-2 72000

Like the *Duke of Gloucester* no ready-to-run model of the 'Clans' (as the Class 6 were more commonly known) is available, but in 4mm scale MTK market a superstructure kit for fitting on to a Hornby 'Britannia' chassis.

Numbered between 72000 and 72009 this class spent most of its life working on Liverpool/ Manchester-Glasgow/Edinburgh services usually north of Carlisle.

Class 5 4-6-0 73000

Numbered between 73000 and 73171, the 172 members of this class were widely distributed throughout Britain although they seldom appeared on the Eastern Region. Their main area

of work ranging from express passenger to freight were:

(a) The South Eastern and (especially) the South Western Divisions of the Southern Region.
(b) Around Perth and Glasgow; and the West Highland line.
(c) The Midland main line from Leeds to St Pancras.
(d) North West England particularly around Manchester.
(e) Chester, Shrewsbury, and the Central Wales line.

Above: The Class 3 Mogul 2-6-0 as it emerged from the Works. *BR*

Opposite upper: Class 4 4-6-0 — a general purpose loco. *Ian Allan Library*

Opposite centre: A side view of the mixed traffic Class 4 2-6-0 *BR*

Opposite lower: Class 4 4-6-0 used in Scotland and on the Southern Region. *BR*

These locos were coupled to a variety of tenders so it is worth checking from photographs if you are modelling a particular locomotive. Nos 73125-73154 were fitted with Caprotti valve gear and this was the only major variation within the class.

Trix once made a model — to 3.8mm:1ft scale — for OO gauge, while MTK produce a cast metal kit. For TT modellers Bec once made a kit to fit over a Tri-ang Britannia chassis. In N gauge it may be possible to modify the Graham Farish Class 5 4-6-0.

Class 4 4-6-0 75000

For those wanting a good general purpose locomotive available for a wide range of duties on both main and branch lines this type is eminently suitable. In 4mm scale there is a ready-to-run version from Palitoy, although this may be withdrawn, it could possibly be around secondhand.

Regarding the prototype, these locos were allocated to the Southern, Western and London Midland Regions, being particularly associated with the Cambrian Coast line in mid-Wales.

The principal variation within this class again was the type of tender. Of the 80 locos built, the last 15 (Nos 75065-75079) which were on the Southern had the larger BRIB type of flush-sided tender and from 1957 were fitted with double chimneys.

Class 4 2-6-0 76000

Available from Airfix as an unmotorised plastic kit in OO scale, the 115 members of this class (Nos 76000-76114) operated principally at either end of the country. On the Southern Region they were fitted with the larger flush sided tenders (Nos 76053-76069) and were a familiar sight on both the Central and South Western Divisions, especially on secondary cross-country services. In Scotland their main haunts were along the East Coast and in the Central Lowlands.

Class 3 2-6-0 77000

No ready-to-run models or kits are available for this class, but as the chassis is identical to that of the Class 4 2-6-0, it may be possible to modify the Airfix plastic kit.

The 20 members of the class — numbered between 77000-77019 — spent most of their lives

43

on secondary passenger and freight duties on South Clydeside in Scotland and in the County of Durham, Teesside and Darlington areas of North East England.

Class 2 2-6-0 78000

These were the smallest of the standard tender types and were derived from Ivatt's design of the 2-6-0 for the LMSR. The 65 members of the class (Nos 78000-78064) were scattered throughout a large number of sheds with particular con-

centrations at Machynlleth for working on the Cambrian Coast, and at Northallerton and Wigan.

In model form this type can be reproduced by making slight modifications to the Hornby Ivatt Class 2 in 4mm scale. In N gauge there is a Minitrix version.

Class 4 2-6-4T 80000

One of the longest running types of model still in production (in 1981), must be the Hornby Dublo

Above: The popular Class 4 2-6-4T which was based on an LMSR design and the subject of the Hornby Dublo model. *BR*

Left: The smallest of the Standard classes — the mixed traffic and branch line loco — Class 2 2-6-0. *BR*

Lower left: A smaller and insignificant version of the 2-6-4T, this is the Class 3 2-6-2T. *BR*

(now Wrenn) version of this class in OO gauge. In N gauge, about 10 years ago, Lima made for Wrenn a model of this class, but frankly this would not stand comparison with the quality one expects today.

Numbered between 80000 and 80154, about one third of the class was shedded in Scotland where they worked many local passenger services especially on the south side of Glasgow. Elsewhere they worked on the London, Tilbury and Southend line before electrification and on the Central Division of the Southern Region from Victoria to Tunbridge Wells West etc. Passenger freight and empty coaching stock workings all came within their ambit.

Class 3 2-6-2T 82000

This class was mainly concentrated on the Southern Region (especially on the branch lines of East Devon and North Cornwall) and the Western Region.

45

Tri-ang once made a ready-to-run model of this class for OO, but unfortunately this is no longer available. However MTK make a cast metal kit.

Class 2 2-6-2T 84000

Like the Class 2 tender type, this 2-6-2T was derived from its Ivatt LMSR designed counterpart and hence can be reproduced in N gauge by modifying the Minitrix Ivatt 2-6-2T or in OO by converting the Ks kit of the same class.

This type is ideally suited for push-pull on a small layout. The 30 members of the prototype (Nos 84000-84029) operated in many areas, but particularly in North West England and a few in Kent.

Class 9F 2-10-0 92000

The 251 members of this class (92000-92250) included the last steam loco to be built for BR — the famous *Evening Star*. Widely used in South Wales, the East Midlands, Tyneside and on the East Coast Main Line for heavy freight and mineral workings they could also occasionally put their hand to express passenger and summer Saturday extras.

There are many variations within the class, the principal one being the Crosti boiler fitted to 92020-92029. Thus if you are modelling a particular loco it is worth checking with photographs.

Ready-to-run models are available in 4mm scale from Hornby and in N gauge from Minitrix. Airfix also make a 4mm scale non-motorised plastic kit.

BIBLIOGRAPHY

In conclusion, a few words on some useful references relating to BRs Standard classes.

Ian Allan Ltd

Ivatt and Riddles Locomotives by Brian Haresnape is a very good general introduction to the Standard types and if you only wanted to look at one book on the subject this would be it. For those wanting more background information, *British Railways Standard Steam Locomotives* by E. S. Cox (out of print in 1980) is well worth reading. It also contains some useful photographs of the controls in the driver's cab and official photos of each of the classes. *Locomotives Illustrated*, a quarterly publication, has had photo-features (some photos are in colour) on the Standard classes. The relevant ones are No 5 on the 9F 2-10-0s; No 10 on the 4-6-2s; No 15 on the 4-6-0s and No 21 on the Standard tank locos. Some of these may well be out of print when this article is published but again may be obtainable secondhand. *BR Standard Steam Album*, a very good pictorial book with a lot of information in the extended captions.

D. Bradford Barton Ltd

Four albums from the publisher's collection have dealt with the Standard classes and each one has top quality photographs, many in close-up, which are extremely useful. *BR Standard Steam in Action; BR Standard 2-10-0 Class 9F; BR Standard Britannia Pacifics* and *BR Standard Steam in Close-up.*

Profile Publications

Loco *Profile No 12* relating to the 'Britannias' and Loco *Profile No 33* about the 9F 2-10-0s are also extremely interesting if one wants to know more of the technical side and their variations, but these books are now difficult to obtain.

Over the years there have also been many articles in the model press relating to the Standard classes, so it is really a question of thumbing through back issues. One in particular is the January '65 issue of *MRC* for an article on Modifications to the Airfix model of the 9F which also gives details of the variations and the ways to model them.

Opposite: Very similar to the Class 3 2-6-2T is this Class 2 with the same wheel arrangement. *BR*

Below: The long and powerful looking Class 9 2-10-0 the largest locos built for BR. *BR*

Lakeside to Plainfield

An American HO system in Great Britain

DAVID V. DAVIES

Apparently when aged about three years I used to ask to go and see the trains at Cirencester, Watermoor when taken for outings in my pushchair. Perhaps my Father going to war from this station influenced it, or having an unknown Great Grandfather who was a driver on the Taff Vale Railway influenced me, but railways have been in my blood ever since.

At six I was given a clockwork Hornby O gauge, which lasted until a younger Sister took to using the track as a footpath; Later an Ever Ready electric tube train came and went. The interest in the prototype returned while at school in East Devon, when many friends came to school daily by a GWR 14XX 0-4-2T which powered the auto trains. After school I even worked in an office in a builders' merchants between watching the morning train arriving with loads of coal, bagged cement, plaster and even the last wagon load of timber before road transport took over.

So why do I model American? Well model railways as a real hobby did not get going until after my marriage, when the first portable layout was built to fit on top of the piano. Then a bigger house and a bigger Hornby layout, then a relative arrived one day with an American Rivarossi loco. Its running was so much better than I could get with the Hornby locos that the die was cast for the change.

Below: The main buildings of the works of the Consolidated Rock Products which is featured on the layout. The train passing on the right is 'The Hawk'.

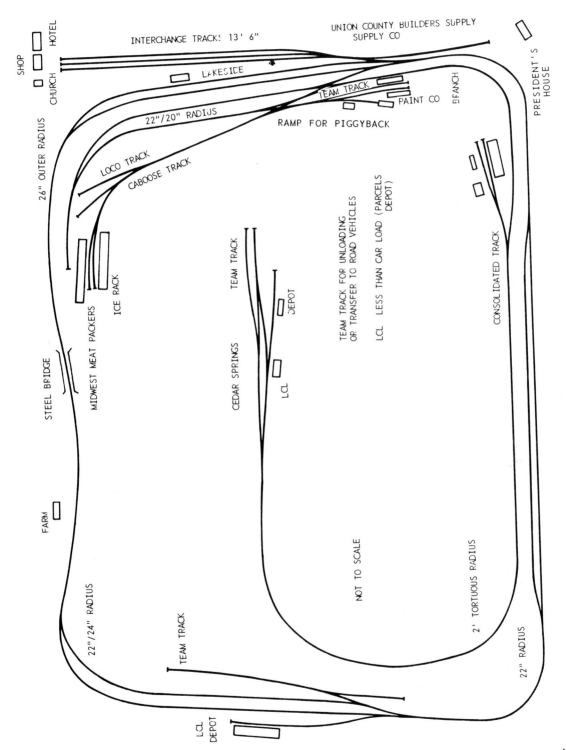

SHOP

HOTEL

CHURCH

INTERCHANGE TRACKS 13' 6"

UNION COUNTY BUILDERS SUPPLY
SUPPLY CO

LAKESIDE

TEAM TRACK

PAINT CO

BRANCH

PRESIDENT'S
HOUSE

26" OUTER RADIUS

22"/20" RADIUS

RAMP FOR PIGGYBACK

LOCO TRACK

CABOOSE TRACK

STEEL BRIDGE

MIDWEST MEAT PACKERS

ICE RACK

TEAM TRACK

CEDAR SPRINGS

LCL

DEPOT

TEAM TRACK FOR UNLOADING
OR TRANSFER TO ROAD VEHICLES

LCL LESS THAN CAR LOAD (PARCELS
DEPOT)

CONSOLIDATED TRACK

FARM

NOT TO SCALE

2' TORTUOUS RADIUS

22" RADIUS

22"/24" RADIUS

TEAM TRACK

LCL
DEPOT

49

Above: No 631 comes up the main line into Lakeside. No 9361, a Baldwin switcher (Athearn model) works the Midwest Meat Packers and the icing plant siding. Before mechanical refrigeration cars were produced, real ice was packed into reefers to keep the contents cool.

Opposite: Two EMD (Electro Motive Division of General Motors) type GP7 with a branch freight train passing the Consolidated Rock Products plant.

Initially the change was slow but the second loco purchased was the Rivarossi Burlington diesel. Suddenly a whole new World to discover, for to model reasonably, accurately information was needed. Books were acquired, North American magazines as well as the British were taken, different suppliers found and the whole ball game of the joy of 3.5mm scale modelling with working Kadee couplers, no buffer interlocking, accurate operation were discovered and the present continuing layout started.

In fact it was started soon after we moved to our present house in 1970. Chosen for its large

attic (among other things), I had a space 17ft 6in long by 13ft 6in wide, with clear head room. The centre of the loft included the chimney and water tank.

Rather than build all the baseboards at once, the main station, built on Sundeala supported by 2in by 1in at 1ft centres across L girders fixed to the rafters, was commenced, sceniced and made operative so some running could be enjoyed. The two hidden sidings followed before the rest of the main line was built on plywood shaped to follow the route, with Sundeala capping supported by short L girders screwed to the rafters.

The girders were at various heights to allow for scenery above and below track levels away from the station areas.

Scenery is built from card formers covered by a lattice of masking tape overlaid with plaster inpregnated bandage. A thin mix of cellulose filler was brushed over to smooth the shapes for a final covering of zip texturing and ground foam.

After various experiments most of the track was laid with Peco and Peco points. The latter are

Above: An EMD type SD7 Switcher on the spur tracks at Lakeside.

Opposite: Marshalling freight cars at Lakeside.

53

Left: 'The Hawk' arrives at Lakeside station.

Overleaf left: 'The Hawk' at Condor Springs.

Overleaf right: Shunting at Plainfield.

gradually being replaced with the Peco Finescale points, which in conjunction with NMRA code 25 wheel flanges, gives very fine smooth running. Rail is painted rust colour, ballast is fine stone, sold for the purpose fixed in place with very diluted white glue. The layout is cab controlled with four Scalespeed controllers driven by two Scalespeed transformers. A separate transformer is for the H&M pointmotors.

The layout is built for operation, the theory being that it is part of a cross country line in the Midwest of the USA. From the small town of Lakeside is a branch to Plainfield. The period modelled is the mid-fifties when diesels on the

Opposite upper: Loco facilities at Lakeside.

Opposite lower: A signal check for No 631. This loco is a Roundhouse kit with extra details, but the wrong valve gear.

Below: An Eastbound freight train for Lakeside crossing a lattice girder bridge over a highway.

Above: Eastbound No 7 'The Hawk'. An E7 (Modelpower model) in Chicago, Burlington and Quincy livery hauls a Railway Post Office car and another coach near Cedar Springs. Such passenger services finished in the late '50s on many minor lines.

Opposite upper: Close-up of uncoupling with Kadee couplers over magnetic uncoupler at Plainfield.

Opposite lower: Close-up of front end of Loco No 631.

Chicago, Burlington and Quincy Railroad (the Burlington) had virtually displaced steam. This cuts out the need for turntables, roundhouses etc which take up so much space I think. A normal operation sequence is an East and West bound passenger train, and East and West bound local (pedlar) freight with connecting passenger and freight along the branch.

Freight train operation is most interesting using a card system. There is a card for each freight car giving car details, also a Perspex pocket into which can be slipped a waybill; a destination order. These take into account car type and destination ie: so a cement hopper does not go to a meat packer, only refrigerator (reefers) cars. So at the beginning of a sequence the cards (for the freight trains) or waybills are sorted and it is the operators intention to get the car to its correct destination. So the train and the layout get the added interest of a chess game.

To get the best of these ideas, reliable operation is essential. Low cost diesels give this reliability more than I seem to get from steam outline locomotives.

The prototype USA railroads buy their locos from outside manufacturers like some of us buy cars. A standard model, but with your own options and choice of colours. So part of the interest is in superdetailing, repainting, decalling the plastic diesel bodies to follow practices of the prototype railroad being modelled. In fact the Burlington had a passenger diesel livery and a different freight livery. The latter changed from

61

time to time and in the late 50s it was possible to see the silver passenger diesels, the early streamlined freight diesels in off white with a red horizontal stripe, the early GP (General Purpose) diesels in black and grey with the latter GPs (known as Geeps) in Chinese red and grey. I have examples of these liveries in use and with the different paint colours and lettering on various freight cars, the whole scene becomes very different from the British Rail scene I had known well since the mid-'50s.

I could not complete this article without reference to the National Model Railroaders Association. Formed in the thirties in the States it has worked and produced standards to which most American manufacturers adhere. Wheel standards, couplers, track dimensions etc are followed, giving the modeller a freedom of inter-change unknown by most European modellers. The British Region meets quarterly with many local groups active throughout the UK. I have learned a great deal from many other members and would recommend membership to all interested in modelling the American way.

Right: Another view of the Consolidated Rock Products plant. All the scenery is edged with shaped hardboard and painted black, as seen in the foreground.

Below: No 631 again, as it coasts down grade with an Eastbound pedlar freight train.

Stock List of Locos in Normal Use

Diesel
2 Athern GP 9s (powered)
1 Athern GP 9 (unpowered)
1 Athern SD 9 (powered)
1 Athern F7 ABA (powered)
1 Model Power E8 (powered)

Steam
1 Model Die Casting Kit 2-8-0
1 North West Short Line 0-6-0

Freight cars are assorted plastic, almost ready-to-run kits, repainted and super-detailed, plus a few wood craft kits. All are weighted at one ounce to the scale 10ft to improve coupler operation and all are fitted with Kadee metal wheels on plastic axles, necessary because of the use of magnetic uncouplers which can affect steel axled cars.

Two brass cabooses of a type introduced in 1889 and still in use in 1970 are used at the rear of the trains.

Scale Plans (7mm : 1ft)

NBR Low sided Dumb-buffered Wagon drawn by K. NORRIS

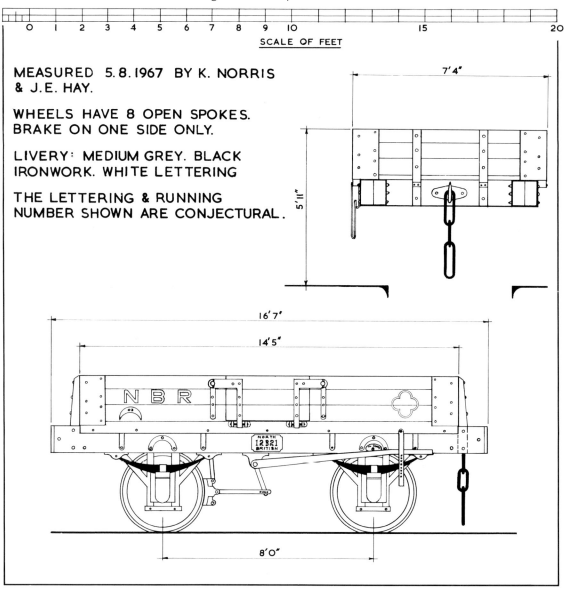

SCALE OF FEET

MEASURED 5.8.1967 BY K. NORRIS
& J.E. HAY.

WHEELS HAVE 8 OPEN SPOKES.
BRAKE ON ONE SIDE ONLY.

LIVERY: MEDIUM GREY. BLACK
IRONWORK. WHITE LETTERING

THE LETTERING & RUNNING
NUMBER SHOWN ARE CONJECTURAL.

Metropolitan Rly 5 plank 10 ton wagon drawn by S. CUNNINGHAM

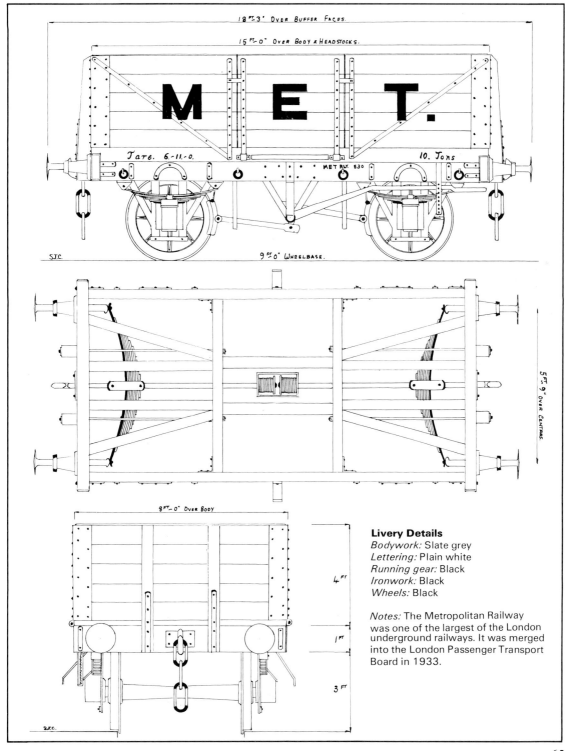

Livery Details

Bodywork: Slate grey
Lettering: Plain white
Running gear: Black
Ironwork: Black
Wheels: Black

Notes: The Metropolitan Railway was one of the largest of the London underground railways. It was merged into the London Passenger Transport Board in 1933.

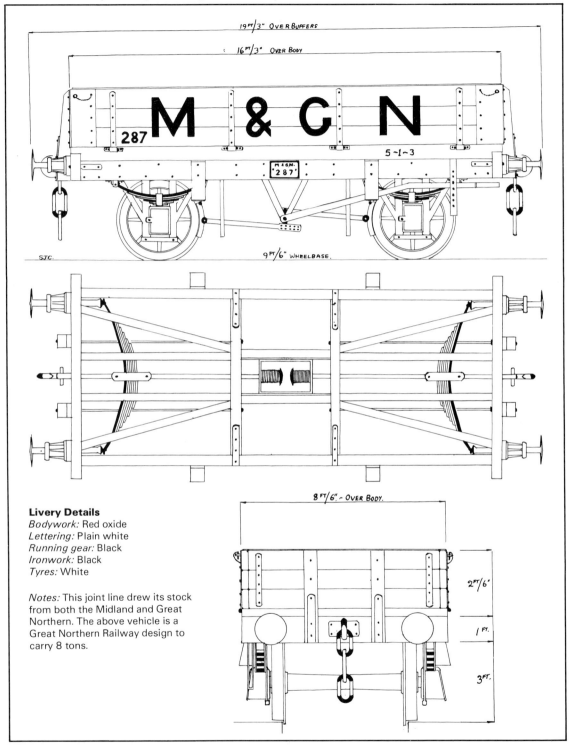

Livery Details

Bodywork: Red oxide
Lettering: Plain white
Running gear: Black
Ironwork: Black
Tyres: White

Notes: This joint line drew its stock from both the Midland and Great Northern. The above vehicle is a Great Northern Railway design to carry 8 tons.

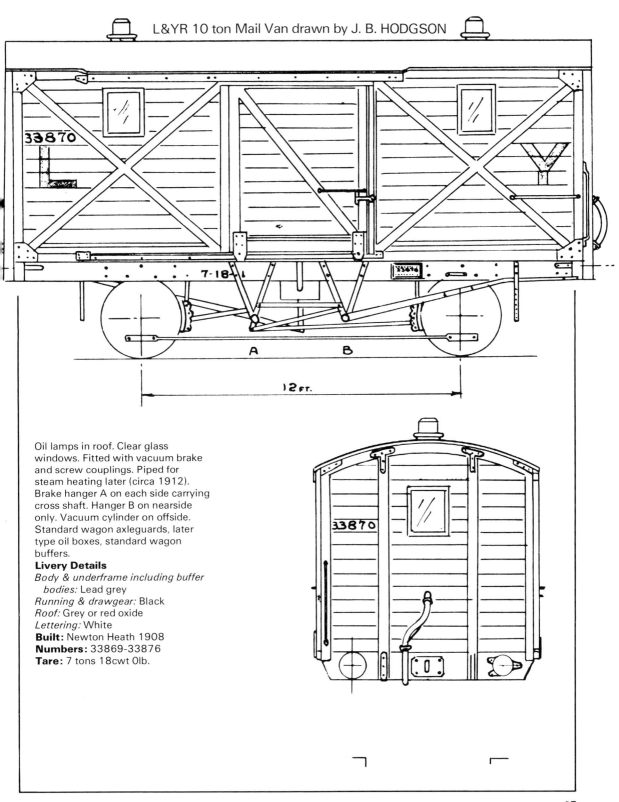

L&YR 10 ton Mail Van drawn by J. B. HODGSON

33870

7-18-1

A   B

12 FT.

Oil lamps in roof. Clear glass windows. Fitted with vacuum brake and screw couplings. Piped for steam heating later (circa 1912). Brake hanger A on each side carrying cross shaft. Hanger B on nearside only. Vacuum cylinder on offside. Standard wagon axleguards, later type oil boxes, standard wagon buffers.

Livery Details

Body & underframe including buffer bodies: Lead grey

Running & drawgear: Black

Roof: Grey or red oxide

Lettering: White

Built: Newton Heath 1908

Numbers: 33869-33876

Tare: 7 tons 18cwt 0lb.

33870

GER 28ft Bogie Tramcar, built 1895. Scale 4mm : 1ft

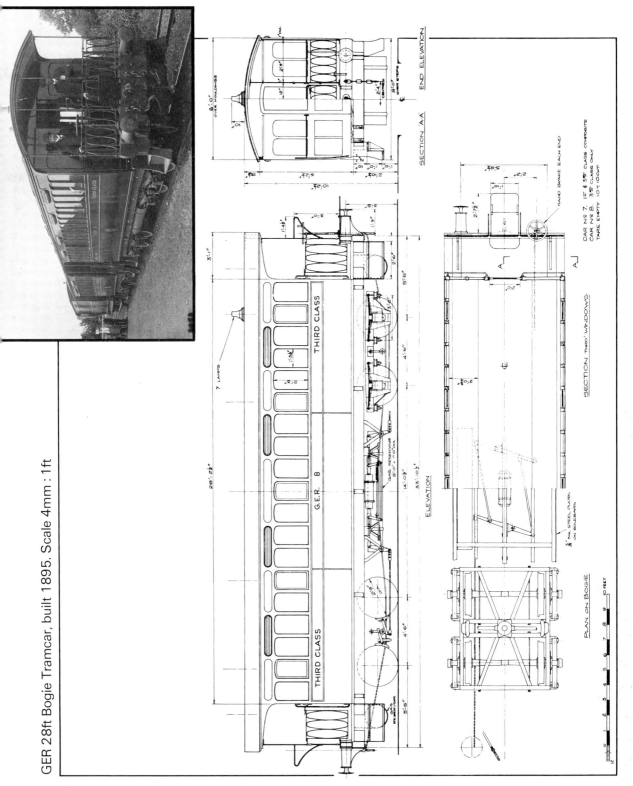

GER 3rd Class Tramcar 1905 for Kelvedon & Tollesbury Branch Scale. 4mm : 1ft

G.E. Numbers 212, 716, 728, 775, 777, 810
G.E. General Arrangement Drg. № 13245B

PART PLAN

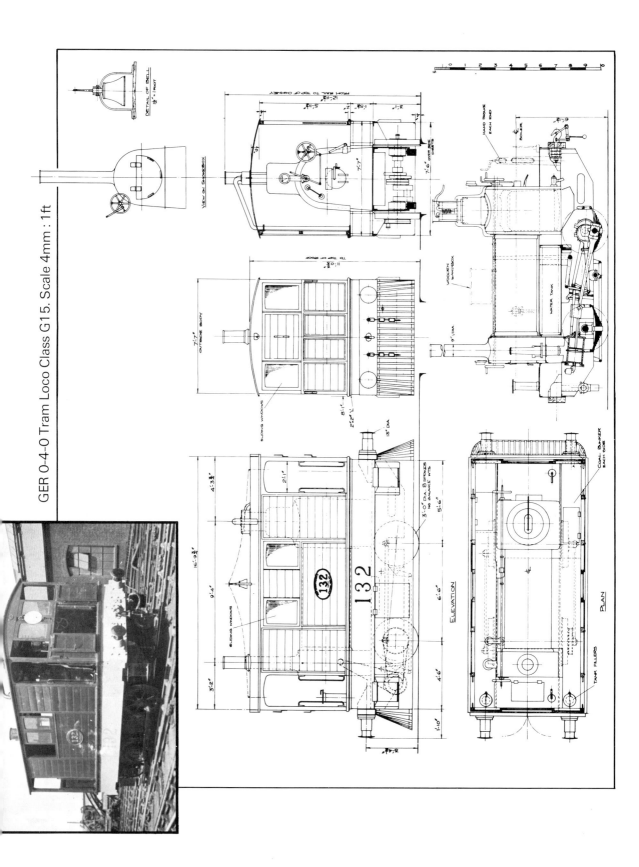

GER 0-4-0 Tram Loco Class G15. Scale 4mm : 1ft

Research into a Railway

ROGER B. POUND

Most of us like to think that our model railway mirrors a real life situation, if it is not based on any particular line, that is to say very broadly freelance in location. It is true to say that most modellers pay particular attention to locos and rolling stock, ensuring the right types appear. However, having been in this marvellous hobby of ours for more years than I care to own to, and having made essays into most of the popular gauges, I have recently consolidated my efforts in to producing a small O gauge system and for once in my life I decided to do a bit of research in depth, and I stress in depth, before building my layout.

I am fortunate in that I live in the East Midlands, where branches abounded at one time. However, to model on the basis of an actual branch did not appeal to me as I doubted my own capabilities to reproduce accurately the inevitable amount of features still extant. Therefore I decided to do a bit of map reading and see if anything presented itself and it did.

Careful pondering over an Ordnance survey map revealed that the River Sence in Leicestershire crosses under the Leicester-St Pancras main line very near to the site of the station (now closed) for Great Glen. Following the river back towards its source led through Great Glen village, crossing the A6 Leicester-Kettering road and on towards a hamlet called Little Stretton. The valley also passed near to the site of the long dead village of Stretton Magna. Slightly north-west of Stretton Magna is what is now known as Leicester East Airfield. This airfield has seen service as a military base and is now the home of the local flying club and is a flourishing field.

With these facts available, it occurred to me that there was sufficient evidence to extend the facts to justify a branch line up the Sence valley, to introduce a new village of Stretton Magna, and bearing in mind the topography combined with a known affinity of the Armed Services for narrow gauge railways, introduce an NG feeder from Stretton Magna to the airfield.

Before I go further, I know that the likely line of a 'branch that never was' has been written about before, so I claim no originality from that point of view. However, having decided the route, it is a good idea to go out and 'look the route over'. One must now decide on the period to be modelled. Having so done, when one does site work, new developments in building can be ignored, but the nature of the land now built on must be discovered as it was prior to building. For example was it farmed or open land? Were there trees there which a railway line would not have interfered with etc, etc? It is most useful to obtain copies, or at least have sight of old large scale (5in to the mile) maps, and place like the local Parish councils may be able to assist in this matter. The Public Library will have a section on local history — check it out, there is sure to be something which will be of help. Local Historians are, fortunately, usually most willing to get in to print!

A day out with a camera is invaluable. Photographs of the present day scene combined with information from old maps is a great asset when building starts.

Thus one can build a branch quite feasibly, or, taking the matter logically forward, divert a main line! Railway buildings, locos and stock require considerably less research in the case I have instanced. It is common knowledge, usually, what classes of locomotives were common in the area and the type of branch envisaged would dictate its own maximum motive power. After all, one is more likely to see a 4F on the branch than an 8F or a Garratt. Railway buildings were fairly standard in design among the larger companies, each company having its characteristics which can be incorporated in a model.

I hope I have shown that there can always reasonably be a reason for YOUR railway having been built - and I can tell you that there is a lot of enjoyment to be had in researching. Just a final cautionary note — do not enter any land where there is no public access without first obtaining proper permission so to do. This simple rule can ensure your safety and freedom from trouble. In the event of permission being refused do not take the law into your own hands — improvise with further research.

Tunnels

An MRC Annual Photo-feature

Above: A scene on the 4mm scale North Devonshire Railway of Ken Northwood as it was c1970. The tunnel is well placed amidst convincing scenery. *Brian Monaghan*

Opposite: Two tunnel portals serve lines on different levels as they pierce the Blackhill Downs on the 4mm scale layout of Howard Lobb. *R. Gordon Taylor*

Below: Another view of the North Devonshire Railway as *King William III* emerges from a tunnel (over which is the watertank in the loft). The build up of the hill to the right is quite realistic. Incidentally the loco is an old Graham Farish model super-detailed and fitted with a Pittman motor. *Brian Monaghan*

Opposite: High Tor tunnel with a high cutting on one side is on the 4mm scale layout of R. G. M. Quarrie which keeps to realistic GWR operation. *Brian Monaghan*

Top: Several single lines tunnels are not unknown on the prototype, and this is the 3.5mm scale Continental layout of Roland Balderstone. The main lines are curving round the mpd. *Brian Monaghan*

Above: A tunnel on a OO gauge layout once owned by the late Harrogate MRC. An LNER Class J50 emerges with a mineral train. *Ron Prattley*

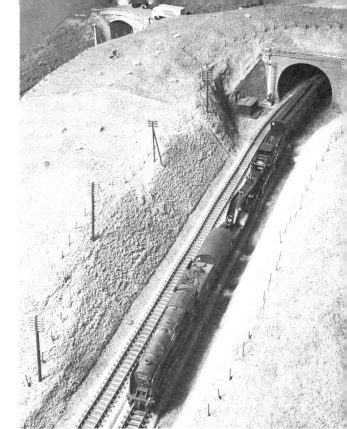

Opposite: A closer view of the three single line tunnels shown on the preceding page situated on the layout of Roland Balderstone. *Brian Monaghan*

Right: Plain scenery with a cutting getting deeper before the tunnel portal is well depicted in this view of a 4mm scale layout of the Sutton Coldfield MRC. *Brian Monaghan*

Below: Rough hewn rock is depicted on the left of the tunnel portal on the OO gauge layout of the late Harrogate MRC. *Ron Prattley*

Why not add an Incline?

DAVE ROWE

On the Thomas Slate Quarry section of my Milkwood Railway there are working models of two inclines, the prototypes for which can be seen at Aberllefenni in Gwynedd. At a recent exhibition one incline needed attention and I realised that many exhibitions had elapsed since the last time it required adjustment, so I thought that I would be safe in recommending an incline as a well tested novelty feature for a layout.

Now it is obvious that few readers will at this point be shouting with excitement 'Great! I was going to build a model slate quarry soon,' but the methods of construction described here could be used to model a cliff railway, examples of which are to be found from Bridgnorth to Bournemouth. In fact I have seen model railways with roads far too precipitous for vehicular traffic and in such situations a cliff railway could look appropriate and add an interesting feature.

The first job I tackled was the making of the winding drum and I turned a piece of heavy broom handle to the shape shown in (A) and then scribed the horizontal lines to simulate the planking of the original. I enjoy lathe work but there is

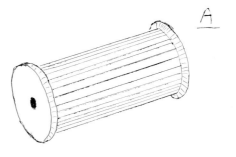

Left: A typical quarry incline with a loaded truck going up and an empty coming down. This is a scene on the Thomas Slate Quarry section of the author's well-known Milkwood Railway.

79

B SECTIONAL VIEW

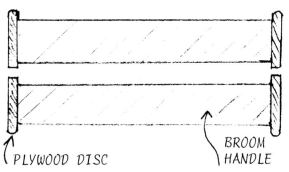

PLYWOOD DISC

BROOM HANDLE

no need to use such equipment as the same effect could have been obtained by using a slightly thinner piece of broom handle and mounting a plywood disc at either end as in (B). My first thought was that it would be difficult to drill the hole truly central without a lathe, but this problem can be circumvented by drilling the hole to say twice the required diameter and then drilling two holes of the correct diameter in the plywood discs and then carefully gluing them in place. A simpler idea might be to cut one end off

C

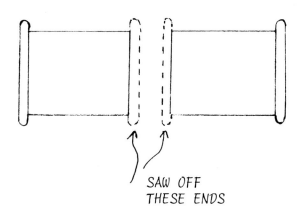

SAW OFF THESE ENDS

each of a pair of cotton reels and then join them together (C). A quick test has shown that the modern plastic reels can be joined with polystyrene cement.

Next I needed a pair of switches to stop the motor when either truck reached the top of its

track. Believing that a crude switch is far more reliable than 37 electronic components assembled together to do the same job, I made the unit shown in (D).

D

COPPER STRIP TOUCHING END OF BENT RAIL (NARROW TIP PROTRUDES BETWEEN SLEEPERS ON INCLINE TRACK)

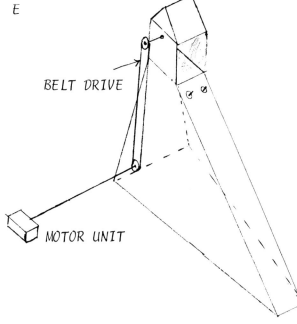

PIECE OF BENT RAIL

WOODEN BLOCK

TO DIODES

FROM DPDT SWITCH

The basic shell of the structure was made from $\frac{3}{8}$in plywood, the various pieces being roughly pinned and glued together as the important thing was to obtain a rigid structure, the finish of this woodwork being unimportant as it would all be

E

BELT DRIVE

MOTOR UNIT

hidden later. The two switches were built in, each copper strip protruding through a $\frac{1}{2}$in hole in the trackbed (E).

Trackwork is not my forte, but even I do not make such a mess of it as the photographs would indicate. The sleepers on the real incline were of various lengths and widths and seemed to have been thrown down and spiked to the rails as they lay. On the model these sleepers were hacked from a sheet of printed circuit board, Evo-stuck in place and the rails soldered on to a scale 4ft gauge. As no electricity was involved there was no need to make an electrical break in the copper.

The two trucks were made from styrene sheet and travel on N gauge loco wheels. A couple of pieces of sheet lead were stuck under each truck to ensure that it descended when required and that the thread was kept taut in a realistic way while they were doing so.

Messrs Meccano supplied a couple of pulleys, a driving band and a long and a short axle so that the drive arrived at the winding drum from a motor which was in a readily accessible position at the rear of the layout. The Hornby turntable mechanism consists of a small motor with a double worm reduction gearing and one of these was pressed into use as the driving unit. There is a 20:1 gear followed by a 40:1 gear — a total

reduction of 800:1 which gives a final drive speed which is ideal for an incline drum.

In the wiring diagram the right hand truck is at the top and the switch has opened. No current flows through the left hand switch and diode until the DPDT switch is thrown to reverse the current. When this happens the left hand truck will ascend until its reaches its switch. The speed of travel can be reduced by inserting a fixed resistor in the line. The diodes should have a rating in excess of the maximum output of the transformer, ie: if the transformer will deliver a maximum of $1\frac{1}{2}$amps the diodes should be able to handle 3amps so that they will survive a short circuit.

I found it necessary to attach the thread just above the line of the axles on the trucks so that when the copper strip on the incline switch struck the axle it did not cause the rear of the truck to be lifted (as it did when the attachment point was too high).

On the Milkwood Railway the DPDT switch is in fact a relay which is operated from time to time by the quarry 'Brain Box'.

The incline was given its finishing coat by applying a liberal coating of grey tinted PVA glue between the rails and sprinkling on a layer of small pieces of shale.

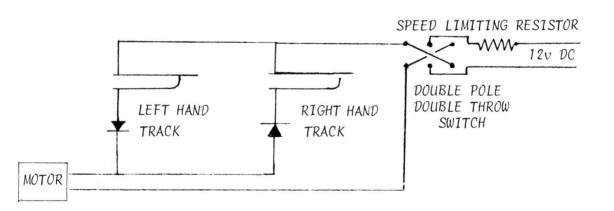

The 'Dukedog' Project

Rebuilding a kit

RAYMENT KIRBY

In its original kit-built form the subject of this article started life normally enough. For a variety of reasons the locomotive never ran on a layout and then it became somewhat damaged after a short encounter with the GPO. From then on the next few stages of its life were all downhill. Sadly on the track it performed in a heavy-nosed way with a pronounced duck-like waddling motion. The white metal body was relegated to the lowly function of being a basis for painting and lining experiments and various mechanical bits were pirated from its mechanism for use in other locomotives. However this is no horror story and better times were ahead.

When the Bluebell Railway wheeled their own *Earl of Berkeley* out into the air after a stay in a rather narrow, gloomy shed, the sight of this — the real thing — provided the inspiration for the rebirth of the model, and so it came to be rebuilt.

The rebuilding seemed in prospect to offer some rather interesting possibilities, so it was not really a question of just putting the loco together again. In its original form the principal defect was a lack of satisfactory performance, some of this could be overcome by altering the mechanics and the rest by readjusting the balance of the loco. The thinking behind this suggested that as most of the loco's weight was over the front drivers they would surely be the best place for directly applying the power, instead of on the rear set, as the kit was designed. Gearing is another matter and a personal choice at that. Each move that is made away from current practice usually produces a certain amount of head shaking and muttering from the pundits — in this case it was suggested that the drive to the front axle would cause the whole loco to revolve on to its nose when power was applied. As this was one of the horrors the rebuilding project was trying to avoid, lowering the gearing, besides its other virtues, in

Below: The model as it was before the restoration — a sorry sight!

Above: The model re-built and ready for the road.

fact made this less likely to occur. And as a bonus the loco would no longer have the acceleration of a dragster. So much for theories — it was then necessary to put them to the test.

The first job was to scrap the original drivers and chassis. It was then discovered by a certain amount of nail biting and drawing on the backs of envelopes that if the motor — a larger K's — was merely reversed it would stick out into the cab. To overcome this a smaller motor would be required and a search produced the ECM unit. This only measures about 17mm by 13mm by 23mm and seemed ideal. The gearing, it was decided, could be a standard 40 — 1 Romford plus an additional 2-1 spur set producing on the track an 80-1 reduction. The chassis (a 2in square block of brass) was duly drilled for the axles and drive shaft and a slot was milled out in the front to accommodate the gears. Home-made 20 and 40 tooth gears were produced on a small lathe after a few anxious moments and many cups of strong tea. The worst part of this was meshing the gears — with this extra 2-1 reduction there had of course to be an extra shaft. This was placed ahead of the front axle towards the top of the chassis block. It was necessary to position this rather carefully, so that the small 20 tooth gear meshed with the 40 tooth one and the drive axle. When this was satisfactory this extra shaft was fitted with the 40 tooth worm wheel which then had to be keyed firmly to the 20 tooth gear. The motor shaft then required sleeving to fit the worm and a mount was made to attach the unit to the chassis. It is now possible to buy these items from the suppliers of the motor, but word of this had not penetrated the woods where the Dukedog was

being refurbished at the time. The mounting system actually made for the motor consisted of a back and front support that fitted over the circular boss forming the motor's armature bearing front and rear. The front support was silver-soldered into a slot cut into the chassis block with a small bolt-on tag on top that fitted into a recess in the motor body, preventing it from revolving in moments of exuberance. The rear support was made L-shaped and bolted to the chassis with an 8BA screw. By making the opening for the armature in the front support U-shaped, and my means of the screw on the back support, a degree of adjustment was provided for worm-meshing had the original sums been a bit out. The current feed was taken through a hole under the motor drilled down to a copper clad strip of plastic screwed to the bottom of the chassis block. This then provided a base for a conventional current collector.

It was decided to use some surplus Hornby Duchess wheels for the new unit as they were of correct diameter. In their original form they were a bit wide and the flanges were not quite what was required, these things were put right on the lathe after another session of strong tea and anxiety. However, all went well, and when one side was bushed with Tufnol insulators the whole

83

mechanism started to look more business-like. The original cranks and axles had been retained but the rods needed replacing. These were made up, flutes cut and the whole unit tried on the track. In spite of its gearing reduction of 80-1, the chassis had a fair turn of speed, perhaps because more use could be made of the higher end of the motor's performance; slow speed performance seemed fairly useful too. An added bonus of course was the power that was developed. The

Above: Another view of the completed model — some of the backhead detail can be seen.

Left: The motor gears and chassis with the tender chassis.

Below left: The new chassis block.

thened by partially filling with glass fibre paste. When the boiler and smoke-box were reassembled and the various fittings replaced by brass turnings, the whole thing became more balanced. The fire-box needed some of its inside removed as the ECM motor is fatter than the K's unit and therefore a fairly tight fit. The original spectacle plate and boiler back plate were replaced by nickel silver ones to make more room. The addition of brass buffers and vac pipes completed the body.

The front bogie required some attention as the original wheels were too small, Larger ones (14mm) necessitated larger clearances being cut in the bogie castings. This destroyed the front beam which caused no loss of sleep, as it had not been fitted with any guard irons. The new nickel silver and brass ones had these features and it improved the look of the bogie somewhat when fitted. As the wheels were now larger, there was a chance of them fouling the bottom of the body under the smoke-box in certain conditions. To stop any electrical fireworks if this should happen, a sheet of Plastikard was cemented to the area of the body at risk.

Finally, there was the question of the tender. This required very little attention. It did need new wheels as the old ones seemed to have got lost somewhere along the way. These new wheels had to have new bearings as the white metal ones seemed rather tired and the holes had become too large for the pinpoint axles. Brass inserts fixed inside the tender frame made things right and located the tender to its correct relationship with the locomotive. The two cranked standards were remade in brass and the white metal drawbar hook was replaced with a steel and nickel silver effort so that the loco and tender had a more sporting chance of staying together. A load of coal and some brass buffers completed the constructional side of the whole project. Painting was by conventional spray methods and the number plate was photo-etched.

Contrary to the cries of the multitude, the extra low gearing has not produced a locomotive that takes hours to travel a few feet. It is of course stately compared with some of the proprietary speed record breakers, but it is both powerful and easy to control. The rebuilding seems in a curious way to have enabled the locomotive to discover something of its own character.

limiting factor in making use of this was obviously going to be the well-known 4-4-0 traction problem.

The body therefore was now going to be an important factor. As built it was, as previously mentioned, very nose-heavy and required some of the tender weight bearing down on the drawbar to keep the rear drivers firmly on the track. Some way was needed to bring the weight back to the rear of the loco. So the boiler and smoke-box were removed and the latter hollowed out as much as possilbe. The white metal boiler barrel was replaced by a thin walled copper one, streng-

Special Trains
Prototype running on an Irish layout

S. J. CARSE

'In connection with above the following special arrangements will apply'. This wording can be seen on many of the circulars issued for special occasions on my Donegal Railway, about 25 being issued each year. The planning of these can be quite simple as in the case of Turf from Derg Bridge to Stranorlar, or complex as in the case of the Orange demonstrations on 12 July, or the Hibernians on 15 August. In general the Orange demonstrations tend to be held in the same venue each year, while the Hibernians hold their demonstration in a different town each year, sometimes outside the County Donegal Railway area altogether.

The prototype of my line, The County Donegal Railways (3ft gauge) was situated in the North West of Ireland and ran between Strabane and Killybegs, with a branch from Donegal Town to Ballyshannon. It also worked the Strabane and Letterkenny Railway, and the Strabane/Derry branch of the LMSR-Northern Counties Committee (NCC).

As it is now closed it is not possible to copy exactly their arrangements as was done before closure, so that they are planned on a combination of (a) What the Railway did in the past; (b) What the road service did last year and (c) What traffic the railway could expect if still open.

Above: Loco No 6 and train near Stranorlar up distant signal. *Sean Kennedy*

Opposite: Railcar No 15 passing McNamee's gates. Note the van being pulled behind the railcar. *David Carse*

When we come to consider the 12 July 1973 arrangements it was found that two venues were involved, Dromore Co Tyrone and Portstewart, Co Derry. Therefore the following movement of passengers was expected. Killybegs to Ballyshannon for transfer to Dromore by road bus; West

Donegal line Stranorlar to Donegal Town to connect with above; and Stranorlar and Strabane to Derry for transfer to Portstewart by Northern Ireland Railways broad gauge train.

On a small line with limited rolling stock, the first thing that must be done when planning special services is to see what spare rolling stock is available and then deploy it in position the day before (ie the previous tracknight). Our steam coaching stock comprises 16 vehicles viz 11 coaches and 5 vans (passenger Compts Guard). Of these, two vans and one coach are required on the regular goods and mixed trains, and one coach and van on the Strabane/Derry passenger, leaving nine coaches and two vans spare. Of the six locomotives, two are normally spare, but as No 4 was unfit for service, only one was spare. Six Railcars and the tractor were also available but none spare.

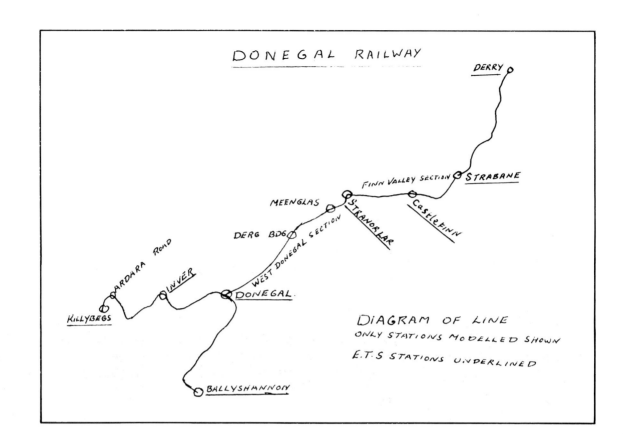

DONEGAL RAILWAY

DERRY

Finn Valley Section
STRABANE

Meenglas
STRANORLAR
Castlefinn

Derg Bdg

West Donegal Section

Ardara Road

Inver

DONEGAL

Killybegs

BALLYSHANNON

DIAGRAM OF LINE
ONLY STATIONS MODELLED SHOWN
E.T.S STATIONS UNDERLINED

Above: Situated on the Barnesmore Bank part of the layout are Railcars Nos 14 & 15 with coach No 40 and some wagons at the rear. Part of Strabane station is on the lower level. *David Carse*

Opposite: Railcar No 19 comes under a bridge in a cutting near Meenglas. *Sean Kennedy*

Before going on to the arrangements some notes on the locomotives will be in order. The four regular engines are home built, from sheet tin, and are as follows;

No 2 Class 5A 2-6-4T *Blanche* This is the most powerful locomotive on the line and is powered by a MW 5-pole motor.

No 5 Class 5 2-6-4T *Drumboe*.Almost as powerful as the class 5A it is powered by a Tri-ang motor.

No 11 Class 4 4-6-4T *Erne* powered by motor ex Hornby diesel shunter. Very powerful on level, but not as good on banks. These locos rotate and are shedded at Strabane and Stranorlar in turn.

No 6 Class 2 4-6-0T *Inver* This is a model of one of the older locos, powered by a Hornby motor. It works on the Strabane/Derry branch, and is painted in the earlier Donegal Railway livery of green.

No 9 *Eske* a Tri-ang 4-6-4T (Indian type rebuilt) and No 4 *Meenglas* a Hornby 0-6-2T are spare and fill in when required.

It is hoped that the addition of a Class 3 4-4-4T, and another Class 5, will render them redundant in the near future. The prototype of the tractor (No 11 in the railcar series) came to the CDR from the Clogher Valley Railway, and is now preserved in the Transport Museum in Belfast. The model, like all the railcars, is powered by a

Above: Stranorlar station and a more general view of the layout with Railcar No 10 and loco in the yard. Loco No 6 is on a mixed train at the station platform.
Sean Kennedy

Walker-Romford flywheel drive motor bogie, and spends its time shunting in Strabane.

In the following, the times shown are as on my timetable with the prototype times in brackets. To cover the 8.21 Killeybegs/Ballyshannon special, four coaches and a van were sent to Killeybegs the previous day as follows. A steam train was substituted for the railcar on the regular 8.40 (11.20) Strabane to Killybegs to cater for a party

of school children travelling to Teelin college, and this left three coaches in Killybegs. Another coach was required on the 9.0 (14.20) Strabane/Killybegs railcar, and this provided the fourth coach. The loco and van were obtained by cancelling the 9.0 (14.00) Killybegs/Stranorlar goods and stabling the loco in Killybegs instead of Stranorlar. This special worked to Donegal at 8.21 (08.21), thence working the regular 8.24 (09.27) Donegal/Ballyshannon. On the return journey the special worked in the path of the regular 9.31 (19.05) ex Ballyshannon and the 9.33 (20.10) Donegal/Killybegs.

For stations Stranorlar/Donegal, the regular 8.18 (08.23) Stranorlar/Donegal railcar was

The Stranorlar/Derry Special was much more straightforward, worked by steam, four coaches and two vans, it left Stranorlar at 8.18 (09.05) and returned at 9.26 (17.25). On checking our coaches we find that the position is:

	Coaches	Vans
Killybegs/Ballyshannon special	4	1
8.18 ex-Stranorlar and 9.33 ex-Donegal	1	—
Ord. Strabane/Derry services	1	1
8.16 (ord) ex-S'lar and 9.10 ord ex-Strabane	1	1
8.18 Stranorlar/Derry special	4	2
	11	5

A coach and van was allocated to the 8.16 ex-Stranorlar but this was reduced to coach only, as it was found that no van was available for the 8.35 (11.15) goods only Stranorlar/Strabane.

Very little disturbance of the locomotive and railcar rosters were required. The 9.25 (09.51) goods only Stranorlar to Killybegs and its return working, the 9.00 (14.00) ex-Killybegs were cancelled to provide a loco for the Ballyshannon special the loco working to Killybegs the previous night as already explained. The spare Stranorlar loco was used on the Stranorlar/Derry special

Next the special circular and loco register is made out and checked to make sure that the regular services are covered as well as the specials. As can be seen a lot of work goes into the planning for such an event, but great satisfaction is derived when everything works out on the day. The diagram will help readers to follow the working, only the stations modelled are shown.

Since I began to write this, a new challenge has arisen in the form of a new public holiday, 1 January. As there was no precedent for this, a service was planned entirely on the special road bus services for that day. This was interesting to work out as the services between Donegal and Ballyshannon and some between Stranorlar/Donegal were part of the through Derry/Sligo service. Five railcars were required to work it, and turned out to be a most interesting timetable. The normal steam service was retained on the Strabane/Derry branch which as a matter of interest has the same service since it was introduced, when the branch was added to the layout some 14 years ago.

strengthened by the addition of an extra railcar and coach, the coach being attached to the Ballyshannon special at Donegal, and detached there on the return journey. As the 9.33 (20.10) regular Donegal/Killybegs was covered by the special steam train, its railcar and the assisting car off the 8.18 ex-Stranolar, formed a special at 9.40 (20.15) from Donegal to Stranorlar, for the return of the West Donegal line passengers.

To provide for the extra railcar on the 8.18 ex Stranorlar the tractor was sent from Strabane the previous night and worked the 8.16 (08.30) Stranorlar to Strabane. The return working of this the 8.22 (09.50) Strabane to Stranorlar was cancelled.

Church Fenton

An ex-NER Junction station

C. T. GOODE

Opposite upper: The 11.15 Leeds-York dmu arrives at Church Fenton in December '68. *M. Mitchell*

Opposite lower: Looking south along the down Sheffield platform.

Top: A general view looking north from the Sheffield platform side.

Above: A view of the platform canopy on the Leeds platform.

Ulleskelf, Bolton Percy, Sherburn-in-Elmet, Church Fenton, all sonorous names and all within a few miles of each other near York and at one time all station names on the route southwards from that most interesting city. The route in question was that of the old York and North Midland Railway, one of the oldest in the country, which was opened in 1839 and which crossed beneath an even older Leeds-Selby Railway of 1835 at Milford Junction where connecting spurs were soon added to the eastern side of the right angled crossing to link the two. North of Milford Jc was Church Fenton, from which point the Y&NM constructed a line running generally north-west via Tadcaster and Wetherby to Harrogate in an attempt to syphon off the London traffic which was going by way of

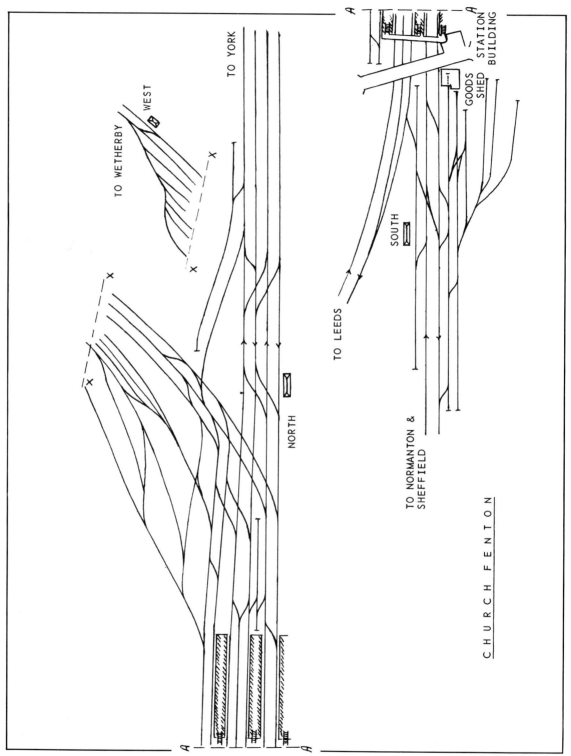

TO WETHERBY

WEST

TO YORK

X

X

NORTH

X

X

A

A

TO LEEDS

SOUTH

TO NORMANTON &
SHEFFIELD

STATION
BUILDING

GOODS
SHED

A

A

C H U R C H   F E N T O N

George Hudson's line through Leeds and Normanton. The line was opened in three sections, that from Church Fenton to Spofforth in 1847, and the remaining $4\frac{3}{4}$ miles of heavier engineering to Harrogate in the following year. At Wetherby a triangular layout brought trains to and from the east side of Leeds. The $18\frac{1}{2}$ mile line never attracted much local custom, apart from during the war years. The outlet faced south and could therefore take trains directly from the Leeds, Sheffield and Normanton lines, though not from York without reversal, which was a pity as a direct run might have stimulated commuters.

Church Fenton station was quite a modest affair of two islands and a side platform on the up side, with a bay (No 5) on the outside of the west island from which Wetherby line trains ran. What is interesting at Church Fenton was the impressive series of connections linking the four running lines from York which arrived at the North Junction cabin as down and up Leeds and down and up Sheffield, double junctions giving a chance to change routes here before the

Wetherby line came sweeping in and the platforms were passed. No 5 bay could in fact serve trains for York as well as Wetherby.

South of the station the South cabin dealt with more domestic affairs in the shape of the goods yard on the east side and an up loop. The box also kept an eye on the Leeds line which disappeared behind it, where a centre line through the station rejoined the adjacent running line. However, South box offered a last chance to trains wishing to gain the Normanton line from the Leeds side by providing a handy escape route through a connection over a spur and across a single slip in front of the signalman.

The village of Church Fenton is a small one north of the road and close to the station whose small booking office and parcels office are on the overbridge. From this building an open footbridge sends uncovered railed ramps down to the platforms which have a building on each with a glass canopy. The odd platform on the east side has lost its 'offices' in the last few years, though the wooden wall and window and door spaces survive, looking out rather blankly at the cows in the pasture next door. At the time of writing the station is virtually complete, though the Wetherby branch and many of the elaborate connections have gone. A great sorting out of some of the complications took place in the area round about 1948. The North signalbox still survives to manipulate the junction points from a console, and the spot can still be very busy and interesting at times with heavy summer workings to and from Liverpool, the south west holiday resorts and the north-east, not many of which stop at Church Fenton.

Below: View from the down Sheffield platform.

Locally much wartime traffic was generated by airmen at the nearby airfield, while on the Wetherby branch special trains were run between points in Yorkshire and the munitions factory at Thorp Arch, these continuing until 1958. Race specials to and from Wetherby would also make a periodic impact on station working, and rakes of older coaches would be stored in the sidings on the north-west side of the layout.

West of Church Fenton station were a brick and tile works and a saw mill, while just to the east by the goods yard resided the local vicar in a spacious rectory with a good view of operations.

Below: The platform awning on the up Sheffield platform.

Lower: The booking office on the road bridge, looking north-east.

Opposite upper: The booking office from platform level, looking south-east.

Opposite lower: The booking office looking north-east.

Church Fenton: Activities at the North end, Dec 1951   **Activities at the South end**

Weekdays

am			
7.15	arrival	Slow	ex-Leeds
7.40	dep	Slow	Leeds via Wetherby
8.05	dep		Bradford-York
8.35	dep	XP	Leeds-York
8.36	dep	Slow	Sheffield-York
9.20	pass	XP	Leeds-Glasgow 'North Briton'
9.45	dep	XP	York-Scarborough
10.49	dep	Slow	Leeds-York
11.53	dep	XP	Leeds-Newcastle

pm			
1.08	dep	XP	Leeds-Scarborough
2.28	dep	XP	Leeds-Newcastle
2.54	dep	Slow	Leeds-York
4.44	dep	XP	Sheffield-York
4.48	dep	XP	Leeds-Scarborough
5.20	pass		Leeds-Newcastle
5.54	dep	SX XP	Leeds-Scarborough
6.08	dep	SO XP	Leeds-Scarborough
6.32	dep	Slow	Leeds-Scarborough
7.50	pass	XP	Liverpool-Newcastle
8.06	dep	Slow	Pontefract Baghill-York
8.49	dep	Slow	Leeds-York
10.01	dep		Normanton-York
10.18	dep	XP	Leeds-York
11.23	dep	Semi	Leeds-York

Sundays

am			
3.20	pass	XP	Liverpool-York
8.16	dep		Normanton-York
8.30	dep	Semi	Leeds-Scarborough
11.55	pass	XP	Liverpool-Newcastle

pm			
2.55	pass	XP	Leeds-Newcastle
3.40	dep	XP	Sheffield-York
6.00	pass	XP	Leeds-Newcastle
7.42	pass	XP	Hull-York
8.00	dep	Semi	Leeds-Darlington
9.20	dep	XP	Sheffield-York
10.18	dep	XP	Leeds-Newcastle
11.46	dep	Semi	Leeds-Newcastle

Activities at the South end

Weekdays

am			
7.11	starts		Normanton
7.36	dep	Slow	York-Sheffield
7.54	arrives		ex-York
7.58	dep	Slow	York-Leeds
8.33	pass	XP	Scarborough-Leeds
9.25	dep	XP	Scarborough-Leeds
9.32	dep	XP	York-Sheffield
10.27	dep	XP	York-Manchester
10.30	pass	XP	York-Bradford
11.09	dep SO	Slow	York-Leeds
11.45	pass	XP	Scarborough-Leeds

pm			
12.30	pass	XP	Newcastle-Leeds
1.18	dep	Slow	York-Sheffield
1.29	dep	Slow	York-Leeds
1.51	pass	XP	Newcastle-Leeds
2.25	pass	XP	York-Leeds
3.26	dep	XP	York-Leeds
4.25	pass	XP	York-Leeds
4.40	dep	Slow	York-Sheffield
5.25	pass	XP	Newcastle-Leeds
5.31	dep	XP	York-Manchester
5.34	arrives		ex-Leeds via Wetherby
5.42	dep	Slow	York-Leeds
5.55	pass	XP	Scarborough-Bradford
7.25	pass	XP	York, Crossgates, Leeds
8.53	dep		York-Normanton
9.49	pass	XP	Glasgow-Leeds 'North Briton'
10.05	pass	XP	York-Liverpool
10.35	dep	XP	York-Sheffield

Sundays

am			
5.15	pass	XP	York-Leeds
8.16	dep		York-Wakefield Westgate
10.03	pass	XP	York-Manchester

pm			
12.20	pass	XP	Newcastle-Liverpool
3.40	dep	XP	York-Sheffield
4.05	dep	XP	York-Leeds
5.10	pass	XP	York-Leeds
7.23	dep	Semi	Newcastle-Leeds
7.54	dep		Normanton
9.05	dep	Semi	Scarborough-Leeds
9.20	dep	XP	York-Sheffield
9.55	dep	XP	York-Hull
10.06	dep	XP	York-Liverpool

As will be noted in the 1951 services, there was only one train each way on weekdays on the Wetherby branch. For comparison, here are the departures for the branch and the arrivals therefrom in 1914.

Down	Departures
7.21am	Leeds Slow
8.00	Leeds Fast, Harrogate
10.30	Harrogate Slow, from York
11.52	Leeds Slow
2.15pm	Harrogate Slow
3.47	Leeds Slow
5.35	Harrogate XP from Kings Cross. Sets down only
5.36	Harrogate Slow
6.48	Leeds Slow, Harrogate
7.36	Harrogate XP from Kings Cross
7.46	Leeds Slow, Harrogate
8.42	Leeds Slow, Harrogate
10.10	Leeds Slow

Up	Arrivals
7.37am	Leeds Slow
9.09	Leeds Slow, Harrogate
10.55	Leeds Slow
12.36pm	Harrogate Slow
2.34	Leeds Slow, Harrogate
2.55	Harrogate XP to Kings Cross Takes up only
5.41	Leeds Slow, Harrogate
6.41	Leeds Slow
8.22	Leeds Slow, Harrogate
9.29	Leeds Slow, Harrogate

No service on Sundays. Passengers changed at Wetherby for Leeds or Harrogate.

Below: The east end of the booking office.

Bridges – 2

A Photo-feature from the camera of BRIAN MONAGHAN

Opposite upper: The GWR main line bridge over the River Thames at Maidenhead is well known and has often been modelled in varying locations. This bridge on the North Devonshire Railway of Ken Northwood is loosely based on the one at Maidenhead. The river bank is made from small pebbles, Polyfilla, sand, green flock and paint. *R. Gillanders*

Opposite lower: A small wooden trestle bridge without any guard rails is suitable for a Narrow Gauge line as depicted here.

Above: A long span trestle girder bridge on a layout which belonged to the late Harrogate MRC. The BR 'Britannia' class *Hereward the Wake* and the BR 2-6-4T have both been detailed and repainted. *Ron Prattley*

Opposite upper: This arched girder bridge was painstakingly made from sections of OO gauge rail and is seen on the layout of the Warley MRC. *E. Tennant*

Opposite lower: A Fleischmann model of DB Class 64 2-6-2T crosses a small bridge on the freelance Continental layout of D. Ashcombe.

Above: A realistic stone road overbridge on the 4mm scale 'Dunnock Edge' layout of J. Flann.

Left: A bridge covered with Faller stonepaper (3.5mm scale) on John Spencer's 3mm scale layout.

Below: An N gauge Arch girder bridge on the Continental 'Heidls-Hod' layout of Frank Wilkinson.

Opposite: A high and impressive viaduct on the layout of Thornbury MRC.

Opposite upper: This 4mm scale bridge was constructed from wood with shellacked card facings for the girders and webs by the late Ross Pochin.

Opposite lower: An unusual structure is this five-tiered gallery on the HOn9 layout depicting a part of India by David Carter.

Above: The arch of the bridge in the foreground is based on a prototype at Bolton, while the viaduct in the background is three of the seven arches on the Bolton-Blackburn line. The arch is constructed from laminated balsa wood strip. These structures are on the 4mm scale L&YR 'Rawnook and Holme Branch' layout of A. H. Bastable.

Grunesdorf am Rhein

A compact HOn9 Continental layout

R. C. GREEN

For several years now I and other members of the South Devon branch of the Narrow Gauge Railway Society have been building layouts of narrow gauge railways, mainly for exhibitions. One of the reasons is to publicise the activities of the society and narrow gauge railways in general, and for this purpose a very simple and nearly automatic layout is neccesary. For this reason we invariably have trains continuously running around an oval and abandon all attempts at shunting and other prototypical activities. Our first effort was a 'Rabbit-warren configuration supposedly representing an Alpine layout with real 'Sound of Music' scenery. The trains would burst in and out of tunnels dodging 3.5mm: 1ft miniatures of Julie Andrews, Christopher Plummer and assorted nuns and children!

Below: View of the waterfront, railway station and the town gate at Grunesdorf am Rheine.

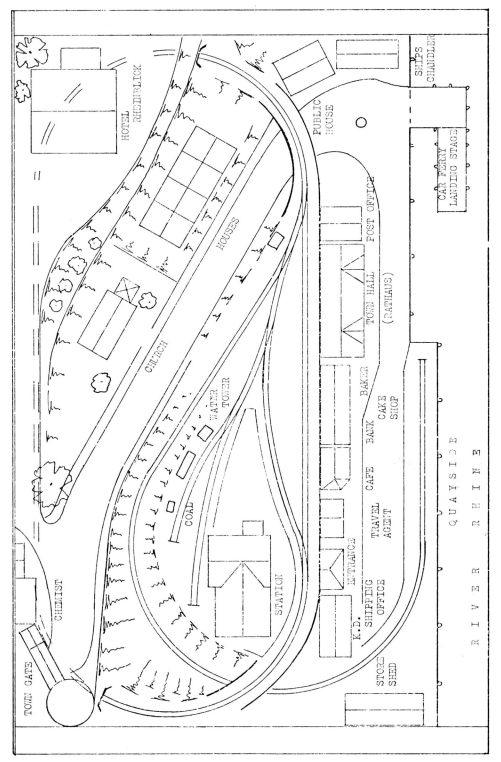

HOTEL RHEINBLICK

CHURCH

HOUSES

TOWN GATE

CHEMIST

COAL

WATER TOWER

STATION

K.D.
SHIPPING
OFFICE

ENTRANCE

TRAVEL
AGENT

CAFE

BANK

BAKER
CAKE SHOP

TOWN HALL
(RATHAUS)

POST OFFICE

PUBLIC HOUSE

SHIPS CHANDLER

CAR FERRY
LANDING STAGE

STORE
SHED

QUAYSIDE

RIVER RHINE

SCALE: 1 to 5

109

After this first layout which was a joint effort, I started work on my own layouts. Following several excursions into the field of Welsh Narrow Gauge Railways I began to tire of converting the Continental rolling stock of Jouef, Eggerbahn and Lilliput into something vaguely Welsh looking. Why not let them run round the track as the manufacturer intended? A trip to the local model railway shop soon revealed that the possibilities in Continental modelling were in some ways better than those in British modelling. Packets of roofs, gutters, windows, shutters, doors, girders and advertisments were available from Faller and these enabled me to make buildings in 3.5mm: 1ft scale with no compromises in dimensional accuracy whatever. By using plastic card for the external walls and sometimes the roofs, and using Faller components for the details, buildings could

Above: Another view of the waterfront, shops, Rathaus and train on the Harbour branch.

Opposite: Looking down the hill past the church and station yard.

be put together which did not have that distinctive look of a commercially available kit.

As I was studying German at evening classes at the time it seemed quite natural to choose a German location — after all, it might improve my vocabulary! A setting on the Rhine would incorporate some water and some hills. A close

inspection of a large scale map suggested a small town on the west bank of the Rhine, somewhere between Bingen and Koblenz, with a narrow gauge line winding its way into the Hunsrück hills. I have subsequently found, while on holiday that lines such as these do exist, although unfortunately they are standard gauge lines. One such is the single track branch to Simmern which leaves the west bank main line at Boppard and climbs out of the Rhine Gorge at an average gradient of 1 20 rising, in places to 1 in 16. In spite of these severe gradients this line is operated by standard Deutsche Bundesbahn diesel railcars employing ordinary adhesive traction. One narrow gauge line still exists at Brohl but is now disused.

The first essential of any German town is the Rathaus, or town hall and this was scratch built

from plastic card except for the gable ends which were from a Faller packet. An Airfix Tarzan, painted in bronze provided the statue of Siegfried, the well known Wagnerian opera hero, above the front entrance. This building is flanked on one side by the Post Office which is painted in the yellow livery of the Deutsche Bundespost and on the other, a row of shops. The shops comprise a Bäckerei (Bakers), a Konditorei (Cake shop and cafe) and a Bezirksparkasse (Savings bank).

One of the problems of small layouts is the treatment of corners. To hide the left hand corner I built a medieval town gate, examples of which are to be found all over Germany. This was built mainly of plastic card embossed with stonework. I found the best method of painting this was to apply a coat of fairly dark matt grey or brown and when dry to rub down with an abrasive

bleach cleaner. This leaves the jointing dark and the face of the stones a lighter shade. The clock faces were obtained from advertisements for wrist watches and clocks in a mail order catalogue. Simply cut them out when there is nobody around to object! The right hand corner contains a hotel which is straight out of the package tour brochure. One of the features of these hotels, and indeed all German housing is the profusion of flowers and plants in window boxes along the balconies. This foliage is easily represented by using crushed brightly coloured plastic sprue. It is surprising how varied the colours available are and by adding small pieces of green foliage from the Britains Tree Kit quite a good impression can be created.

The Rhine is one of the great transport arteries of Europe and apart from a double track main line on each bank, the river itself carries a never ending stream of barges. Some of these are pulled by tugs, some are pushed by tugs and some are self powered. The ship on the layout is converted from a plastic kit of a Russian Trawler. Some of the rear superstructure was removed to increase

Above: Station yard with a train in the bay platform.

Opposite upper: A train hauled by an 0-6-2T drawing into the station.

Opposite lower: A goods train leaves the quayside and passes the shipping office on its way to the main line.

the length of the cargo deck forward of the bridge. The scale is a bit doubtful but this is not readily apparent. As well as the cargo boats there are many passenger carrying ships, some of which are used for short pleasure trips and others which operate a regular service to a timetable. These boats are operated by the Köln-Dusseldorf shipping company. I had contemplated building

114

one of these distinctive ships but they are rather large and in 3.5mm-1 foot scale would have occupied the whole waterfront. I decided to limit myself to building a booking office on the quayside and this can be seen next to the station entrance. This entrance leads via a subway to the main station building at track level. Incidentally the station is one of the two kits that were assembled as per the instructions, the other being the row of four modern houses next to the church.

Many towns on the Rhine which have no road bridge across the river have a car ferry instead. Crossing the Rhine on one of these can be quite exiting as the ferries have to dodge between the barges travelling up and down the river. The effect is similar to being taken across Oxford Street in a perambulator! The ferry on the layout,

The 'St Georg' is made from plastic card. Odd pieces from a Faller packet of girders were used to build the tilting ramps at each end of the ship.

Perhaps a few words about the construction of the layout would be useful. The baseboard and sides were constructed out of an old door. The

Below: At the bottom of the hill.

Opposite: The ferry 'St Georg' unloading in front of the Rathaus.

base measures 4ft by 2ft 9in and the front was cut away to leave a space for the water and to form the quayside. The river is just a piece of hardboard painted a murky green and heavily varnished. The track bed was cut out of one piece of hardboard with a jig saw and then erected on to the baseboard on top of the piers cut from 3in by ½in batten. The track was then laid and tested. When this was satisfactory it was then covered in draughting (masking) tape and the rest of the scenery added, using old bandages steeped in Polyfilla. When the scenery had thoroughly hardened the tape was removed and the track ballasted with granulated cork. The scenery was painted using poster paint. The track used was standard N gauge because I find it easier to lay round sharp curves because it comes in 36in lengths as opposed to the 18in lengths of Peco

crazy track. Also Continental narrow gauge railways tend to look a bit smarter than their British counterparts and the close sleeper spacing is not so noticeable.

The rolling stock currently consists of three Eggerbahn 'Fiery Elias' coaches, two Liliput 'Zillertalbahn' bogie coaches and a few odd Eggerbahn 4-wheelers, all painted in blue and white, and lined with copper. Motive power is provided by a Liliput 0-6-2T and two Jouef 0-4-0Ts. The 0-6-2T was perfectly acceptable 'ex-works', however the Jouefs needed some alterations. The original roofs and supporting pillars were removed and more substantial cabs, made from plastic card, were fitted. Also the boilers were lengthened using pieces of plastic cut from the barrel of an old ball point pen. This means that a new hook has to be fitted at the front of the

117

loco, but this is quite easily done using odd scraps of plastic.

The road vehicles are all of continental prototypes obtained from various manufacturers and are all approximately the correct scale. One gets very queer looks from the management when creeping around a toyshop furtively pulling lorries out of boxes and measuring them against a ruler! One notable vehicle is a Deutsche Bundesbahn Mercedes coach from the Wiking range. This is finished in an old maroon livery of the DB. Currently the buses of the DB are being merged with the yellow Postbus network to from one rationalised system — the Postbahn, the new livery being yellow.

In this article I have tried to show that it is possible to make a model railway which although it is not an exact replica of some particular prototype, is a passable impression of a definite locale. It seems that there are too many of the 'Somewhere in Europe' type of Continental layouts. It is just as easy and much more rewarding to be a bit more precise. Vast quantities of information in the form of brochures, books, maps, etc. may be had from the National Tourist Offices of most countries. These all have addresses in London as do most of the State Railways of Europe who are also pleased to supply literature.

So, after 'Die Hunsrücker Schmallspurbahn', what next? — 'Le Reseau Beaujolais', perhaps?

Opposite upper: The Post Office next to the Rathaus.

Opposite lower: A passenger train draws into the station.

Below: The church and a row of houses with the Hotel Rheinblick on a higher level.

Cold Comfort RPS

The 4mm layout of Tony Osborne

R. CADMAN

The Prototype

Jack Randall was born at Cold Comfort farm in Wiltshire in 1862 and at the age of 21 founded a small quarry on land previously owned by his father. The stone was a rare Wiltshire seam and the business developed rapidly and steady demand kept it flourishing to such an extent that the GWR provided an end extension to the

Nedrub branch line in the late 1890s to handle the traffic generated.

Following the Great War, reduction in demand brought the industry into decline and by the late thirties the original business closed down.

It was resurrected in 1946 by the great grandsons of the founder, Jack and Leslie Randall who opened up a market for a pressed

stone using the spoil from the earlier workings. Not only this but by a unique and highly secret process the by-product, a brown slurry mixture was formed into a synthetic leather from which the world renowned Randall trunks and suitcases are manufactured.

This revival of fortunes came too late to save the branch line which was closed in 1951, but it made millionaires of the brothers who by a happy circumstance of fate were railway enthusiasts.

With their future secure, and time on their hands, thoughts turned to a preservation scheme utilising the trackwork still in existence. This included the branch terminus, a workman's halt at Cold Comfort and the works loco shed.

The idea was not only to preserve locomotives and rolling stock, but also to dismantle and reconstruct as many railway and industrial buildings as possible to recreate the total atmosphere of the period.

The extent to which they have succeeded can be judged from the photographs and the award in 1975 of the Silver Trophy as Britain's principal tourist attraction. In presenting this award Sir Richard Marsh the Chairman of British Rail said that Cold Comfort was to the railway what Portmeiron had been to the world of architecture — a fitting tribute to the enterprise of the Randall

Opposite: A general view of the left hand side of the layout showing the sidings and locomotive repair workshop.

Below: A general view of the right hand side of the layout, overlooking the quarry buildings and the small engine shed.

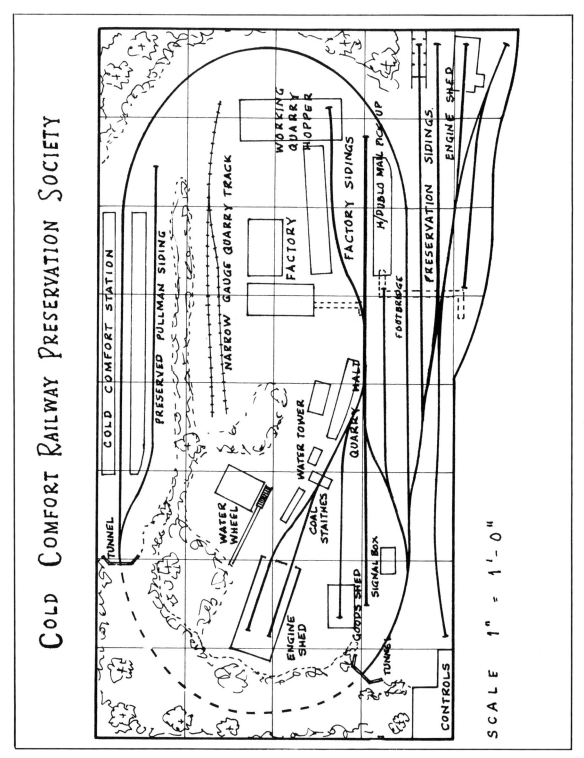

Cold Comfort Railway Preservation Society

COLD COMFORT STATION

PRESERVED PULLMAN SIDING

NARROW GAUGE QUARRY TRACK

WORKING QUARRY HOPPER

FACTORY

FACTORY SIDINGS

H/DUBLO MAIL PICK-UP

FOOTBRIDGE

PRESERVATION SIDINGS.

ENGINE SHED

TUNNEL

WATER WHEEL

WATER TOWER

COAL STAITHES

QUARRY MALT

SIGNAL BOX

ENGINE SHED

GOODS SHED

TUNNEL

CONTROLS

SCALE 1" = 1'-0"

122

Above: The factory with Cold Comfort station in the background. The water mill and power house can be seen at the left hand side.

brothers whose business still flourishes, just, within the confines of what is undoubtedly the finest railway preservation project in the world.

The Model

The prototype history could be the pipe dream of many of us, but it could have happened and the story supports the true history of the model which started life five years ago as the quarry end extension of a GWR branch line.

This was a joint project undertaken by Tony Osborne and John Spencer which floundered some two years or so ago when the rented room that housed it all was reclaimed.

Tony took his 8ft end of the 26ft long layout back to his small bedroom, joined the severed ends of the trackwork into a loop and within a few days the germ of the idea of a preservation scheme layout began to flourish.

The problem was one of that is so familiar to many modellers, lack of space, limited funds, attraction to various prototypes over a wide period, a desire to improve on commercial offerings, a joy of experimenting and last, but by no means least the need to satisfy the desire just to see locomotives in action.

There is also the very particular pleasure derived from taking someone else's scrap or reject and turning it into a satisfactory model. Most of the buildings were inspired from this source with judicious scratch building to complement the overall effect.

The preservation concept was the only one

124

Above: Bulleid Pacific *Dorchester* pulls away from Quarry Halt while Merit commuters show more interest in the offerings of Wymans Bookstall.

Opposite upper: View across the locomotive storage sidings and running lines.

Opposite lower: The quarry head and despatch deck with an order of trunks and suitcases for export to the Middle East.

which satisfied all these conditions and effectively created the nostalgia and atmosphere that steam engines give.

Operation

In operation the layout gives a vivid impression of any one of the several 'big' preservation centres during the annual 'Steam Gala' weekend. There is nothing wrong with the Caley 4-2-2 alongside an A4. Anything is possible, anything can happen — and very often does! its simply a question of 'What would you like to see running?'. This obviously cannot satisfy the single-Company-strict-period-operational man but even he would admit on occasion to a sneaking desire to run at least one engine which appeals to him if only he could find an excuse.

125

This layout needs no excuses, it is a world apart where a man can dream his dreams of days of steam and model what appeals to him at the time or whenever opportunity provides a worthy model for conversion or salvage from the scrap box.

On Construction

One serious objective is to improve the breed and develop modelling skills and techniques. Variations are less apparent in a layout of this kind, which encourages experimentation. The scenery being a case in point, after some trials, with cork and other materials, polystyrene melted with paint and thinners blends down most realistically for final painting and application of flock. Various stages of technique can be seen on the layout which provides a useful lesson for future developments.

Trees are a mixture of lichen, twigs with lichen and flock foliage and some proprietary types.

None of the buildings shown was bought new. All came from rejects and the scrap boxes of various friends. The transformations gave particular pleasure to Tony for with just the right amount of scratch building to make up the differences a very pleasing busy effect has been created which provides a satisfactory background

to the railway activities. The water mill is a working model, even with drought conditions it can be encouraged to produce an adequate supply of water that in theory provides the electricity supply to the quarry and factory.

Locomotives and Stock

The rolling stock is proprietary, some of it being kit built and the origins can easily be identified from the photographs.

Similarly the locomotives are proprietary and kit based but as can be seen they have been super detailed and repainted to conform more closely with the spirit of preservation and the prototype.

The standard of acceptance for Cold Comfort calls for all locomotives to be fully handrailed, moulded handrails being replaced as necessary, vacuum pipes fitted, correct headlamp code, headboards where appropriate and all tenders to be filled with coal. There is no substitute for the real thing!

Nameplates have come from Kings Cross, PC Models and Trueline Models and it is not surprising what a difference they make when applied to a standard Tri-ang loco in place of their usual moulded pattern nameplate.

At present 16 locomotives are preserved at Cold Comfort and having regards to the concept

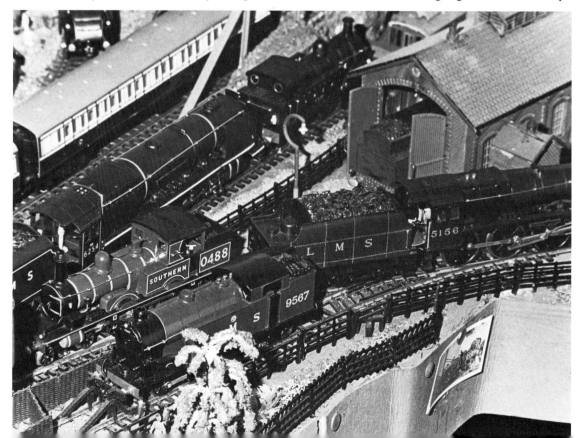

Above: Ex-GWR pannier tank No 8762 with the Ratio 4-wheel stock rounds the quarry head bend with an Open Day Special.

Opposite: A display of locos around the small engine shed.

of the layout it's worth considering one or two of them in some detail.

(1) GWR Pannier 0-6-0PT No 8752 ex-Tri-ang rescued from the bits and pieces box and fully restored. This runs permanently coupled to three Ratio GWR 4-wheel coaches painted in 1901 livery.

(2) 4-4-0T LSWR Adams Radial No 0488. As straight forward a locomotive as you will find on the layout as it has been built from the K's kit without modification.

(3) 4-4-0 MR Johnson No 327. Built from the Ratio kit but with a hand made brass chassis. The original motor was retained and works well with Romford gears and driving wheels. Livery is 1923 LMSR maroon with full lining.

(4) Tony's favourite 'pride of the line' Hornby Silver Seal *Evening Star* with full modifications as outlined above. In addition automatic oiling gear drive has been added and a headboard, LCGB contrived from suitable sized letters from the advertising section of a model magazine mounted on Plastikard and secured in a place with Devcon.

(5) LMSR Class 5 No 5156 *Ayrshire Yeomanry* started life as Tri-ang loco No 45156. Wheels and coupling rods were retained but the Britannia valve gear thrown away and replaced by a handbuilt scale set. The photographs show clearly the improvement and the effect of rivet imprinting on the tender sides.

(6) Ex-Caledonian Railway 4-2-2. The original Tri-ang offering being much improved by the addition of handrailing, under frame detail and painting and lining to colour photo of the original.

(7) Ex LMSR 2-6-0 Ivatt Mogul, one more Hornby loco vastly improved by the addition of a combination lever and small alterations to valve gear.

(8) Hornby 0-6-2T No 9567 preserved in LMSR livery, a 'five bob' rescue from the scrap box. Some may argue about the livery, but it looks nice and preservation societies are a law unto themselves!

(9) Tri-ang 0-6-0 3F No 3776. An early model this, rebuilt from the remnants recovered from a friends scrap box.

Opposite: An Open Day Special at the entrance to the tunnel.

Below: A low level view looking towards quarry head which gives a good impression of the atmosphere created by compressing a lot of railway into a small space.

(10) Tri-ang 0-6-0T *Jinty* also rescued from the scrap box and restored to active service.

(11) Wrenn 0-6-0 LNER Tank engine finished in black and benefiting from an extensive handrailing, rebuild using W&H. Models handrail knobs.

(12) Wrenn 4-6-2 Duchess No 6254 *City of Stoke-on-Trent*. Quite standard except for the necessary repaint.

(13) Wrenn Bulleid Pacific *Dorchester* preserved with Southern number and lettering. Once again artistic license has been exercised, but it certainly looks fine in malachite green.

(14) Wrenn A4 No 60012 *Commonwealth of Australia*. Standard model with rebuilt valve gear and usual refinements to handrails.

(15) Wrenn GWR 4-6-0 *Caerphilly Castle*.

(16) Wrenn LMSR 2-8-0 No 8042.

In all cases the models have been repainted and lined by Tony to apply a consistent standard of finish to the complete range.

In Conclusion

The future of Cold Comfort is secure, there is no shortage of inspiration for future preservation projects the ultimate restriction being lack of space. In the meantime however there is endless pleasure to be had from running trains, planning the next acquisition and simply enjoying the nostalgia of the atmosphere created in having a Company of your own.

The railway end of Dunnock Edge goods shed. The pannier tank loco is a conversion from an old Gaiety kit.
Brian Monaghan